ESSENTIAL POEMS

FROM THE

STAYING ALIVE TRILOGY

edited by NEIL ASTLEY

BLOODAXE BOOKS

ISBN: 978 1 85224 942 7 paperback
        978 1 85224 958 8 hardback

First published 2012 by
Bloodaxe Books Ltd,
Highgreen,
Tarset,
Northumberland NE48 1RP.

www.bloodaxebooks.com
For further information about Bloodaxe titles
please visit our website or write to
the above address for a catalogue.

Supported by
**ARTS COUNCIL
ENGLAND**

*For Pamela and Paul, their friendship,
and for everyone's love and friendship.*

Cover design: Neil Astley & Pamela Robertson-Pearce.

Printed in Great Britain by Bell & Bain Limited, Glasgow, Scotland.

ESSENTIAL POEMS
FROM THE
STAYING ALIVE TRILOGY

'*Staying Alive* is a magnificent anthology. The last time I was so excited, engaged and enthralled by a collection of poems was when I first encountered *The Rattle Bag*. I can't think of any other anthology that casts its net so widely, or one that has introduced me to so many vivid and memorable poems'
— PHILIP PULLMAN

'I love *Staying Alive* and keep going back to it. *Being Alive* is just as vivid, strongly present and equally beautifully organised. But this new book feels even more alive – I think it has a heartbeat, or maybe that's my own thrum humming along with the music of these poets. Sitting alone in a room with these poems is to be assured that you are not alone, you are not crazy (or if you are, you're not the only one who thinks this way!) I run home to this book to argue with it, find solace in it, to locate myself in the world again' — MERYL STREEP

'*Being Human* is…a poetic Babel, a library in one volume'
— ALAN TAYLOR, *The Herald* (Scotland)

'When you choose your book for *Desert Island Discs*, this should be it. *Staying Alive* proves that poetry is the most sustaining and life-affirming of literary forms. A triumph' — HELENA KENNEDY

'The book I'd like to take is called *Staying Alive*…it is 500 wonderful poems… I can learn them off by heart…also I think they will sustain me emotionally while I'm there'
— ANNA FORD on *Desert Island Discs*

'*Staying Alive* is a book which leaves those who have read or heard a poem from it feeling less alone and more alive. Its effect is deeply political – in a way that nobody ten years ago could have foreseen. Why? The 500 poems in it are not political as such. But they have become subversive because they contest the way the world is being (and has been) manipulated and spoken about. They refuse the lies, the arrogant complacencies, the weak-kneed evasions. They offer 500 examples of resistance'
– JOHN BERGER

'Neil Astley's indispensable, endlessly surprising trilogy… The newest and last of these [*Being Human*] contains all the manifold virtues of the earlier two: another startlingly varied, unexpected and entirely accessible collection of contemporary poems – 500 per volume, no small undertaking – exploring the stuff of life, what Louis MacNeice called "*this mad weir of tigerish waters / A prism of delight and pain*"' – CATHERINE LOCKERBIE, *The Scotsman*

'Usually if you say a book is "inspirational" that means it's New Agey and soft at the center. This astonishingly rich anthology, by contrast, shows that what is edgy, authentic and provocative can also awaken the spirit and make its readers quick with consciousness. In these pages I discovered many new writers, and I've decided I'm now in love with our troublesome epoch if it can produce poems of such genius' – EDMUND WHITE

'*Staying Alive* is a blessing of a book. The title says it all. I have long waited for just this kind of setting down of poems – and the way they work together is wonderful – all come together to talk at the same table. Has there ever been such a passionate anthology? These are poems that hunt you down with the solace of their recognition' – ANNE MICHAELS

'A book that travels everywhere with me…It is full of beautiful writing that can blow your mind' – BETH ORTON on *Staying Alive*

'Hopefully, books like this will put poetry back into the mainstream' – VAN MORRISON on *Being Alive*

CONTENTS

INTRODUCTION

Staying Alive, *Being Alive* and *Being Human* have introduced many thousands of new readers to contemporary poetry, and have helped poetry lovers to discover the little known riches of world poetry. With each book in the trilogy already offering the reader 500 essential poems, choosing 100 essential poems for his pocketbook edition from their carefully chosen selections of 1500 poems was always going to be an impossible task.

Staying Alive was never meant to be a definitive anthology of modern poetry, nor was its sequel *Being Alive* or its companion volume *Being Human*. Each was intended to be a helpful guide for new readers as well as a world poetry map showing more territory than most poetry readers would have come across. All three anthologies do of course include some of most significant poems of modern times, but that is not their purpose, so there would have been no point in producing a smaller anthology including just the poems said to have the highest critical standing. This is not a *best of* anthology but a compilation I've made for readers who've wanted a more portable travel companion drawn from the three chunky paperbacks, both in the form of this pocketbook and also as an e-book. I hope it may serve too as a taster for anyone unfamiliar with the individual anthologies.

In drawing up my selection for this condensed edition, I have been especially conscious and respectful of how readers have come to view the three books in *Staying Alive* trilogy as a testifying in a deeply personal way to their own love of poetry as well as somehow validating their relationship with particular poems which have been important to them in their lives.

These anthologies are quite unlike any other books I've edited or published. These are books for which I receive fan mail from people from all walks of life, and the sense I get from the extraordinary correspondence they have generated, and from feedback offered all the time by people who come up to me at events, is that they really *do* have their own following, as if each book were an author with its loyal readership. People don't just read these books and keep them by their bedside, they keep giving them as presents. And so this body of readers grows: all those people out there who see the three anthologies as *their* books, a kind of shared testament to our common humanity expressed in poems. When I edited the third anthology, *Being Human* – and then when assembling this one – I felt an acute sense of responsibility to that readership, a connection with all those people who've put their trust in me to deliver this particular kind of book which they won't just read once but will re-read again and again; and who will feel a special bond with the poems, and will want to share them with others.

Staying Alive is still being discovered by new readers. Ten years on I'm still receiving letters, postcards, phone calls and e-mails expressing people's appreciation, all saying how much *Staying Alive* had helped or stimulated them and fired up their interest in poetry; and then that happened also with *Being Alive* and *Being Human*.

Talismanic poems were a popular feature of *Staying Alive*, notably Mary Oliver's 'Wild Geese' and 'The Journey'. They then became integral to my selections for *Being Alive* and *Being Human*. These are the kinds of poems that people keep in their wallets, on fridges and noticeboards; poems copied to friends and read on special occasions. Such has been the appeal of *Staying Alive* and *Being Alive* that numerous readers wrote not only to express their appreciation of these books, but also to share poems which they had found helpful, empowering or affirming. I drew on this highly unusual publisher's mailbag for *Being Human*, including many talismanic personal survival poems suggested by readers from all walks of life, along with others named by writers at readings and in newspaper articles and blogs. Examples of these include, in particular, poems by Robert Frost, Jane Hirshfield, Langston Hughes and Rilke.

What many of these talismanic poems have in common is a wake-up call to people trying to live meaningful lives in a secular world without certainties, where so much that happens is outside anyone's control, and the individual is pressured to conform to the will of others. And that acquiescence involves not only subservience to dominant political, social or religious codes of behaviour but also submission to capitalism's market-driven, media-pandered consumer society. There are many different kinds of poets represented in these anthologies whose work stands in opposition to those forces and speaks for the crushed or embattled individual, from Ireland's Louis MacNeice to Estonia's Doris Kareva.

Human understanding and intimacy are created not out of imposed order or striving for perfection but through acceptance of difficulty, inadequacy, imperfection, making do, shortage of time, as recognised here in poems by writers as various as Alan Dugan, U.A. Fanthorpe and Jaan Kaplinski. Yehuda Amichai's 'A Man in His Life' concludes: 'A man doesn't have time in his life / to have time for everything.' Warnings against wasting that one life and denying our hopes or dreams crop up again and again in these poems, most famously in Rainer Maria Rilke's 'Archaic Torso of Apollo', which ends 'You must change your life', a call to action which has been picked up by numerous poets as well as by readers taking these poems to heart.

As in the individual anthologies, I have "orchestrated" the selections here in such a way as to bring these kinds of connections between poems alive for the reader, so that poems will seem to talk to one another, with themes picked up and developed through several poems. Given this smaller space in which to present one poem after another, I've tried to give the whole selection a narrative arc, similar to that of the many readings I've done from the three anthologies at festivals and poetry venues over the past ten years. Those readings have been shared with poets, and my selections here include poems they've wanted to read at those events as well as poems which audiences have loved or connected with.

Another popular feature of the three anthologies was my inclusion of brief notes on poets and poems in the short introductions to each section. I couldn't do that for all 500 poems, but I have been able to add comments on the hundred poems in this selection at the back of the book. This is yet one more way in which I've tried to make this anthology responsive to what readers have wanted.

And now it is *your book*, dear reader. I do hope it will travel with you and be a life companion in poems.

NEIL ASTLEY

Wild Geese

You do not have to be good.
You do not have to walk on your knees
for a hundred miles through the desert, repenting.
You only have to let the soft animal of your body
    love what it loves.
Tell me about despair, yours, and I will tell you mine.
Meanwhile the world goes on.
Meanwhile the sun and the clear pebbles of the rain
are moving across the landscapes,
over the prairies and the deep trees,
the mountains and the rivers.
Meanwhile the wild geese, high in the clean blue air,
are heading home again.
Whoever you are, no matter how lonely,
the world offers itself to your imagination,
calls to you like the wild geese, harsh and exciting –
over and over announcing your place
in the family of things.

MARY OLIVER

from Shape of Time

You aren't better than anyone.
You aren't worse than anyone.
You have been given the world.
See what there is to see.

Protect what is around you,
hold who is there beside you.
All creatures in their own way
are funny –

and fragile.

*

The question isn't
how to be in style
but
how to live in truth
in the face of all the winds?

With mindfulness, courage,
patience, sympathy –
how to remain brave
when the spirit fails?

*

Idleness is often empowering,
recreating oneself –
just as the moon gradually
grows full once again,
a battery surely and
steadily recharges,

so everything, everyone
must have time for the self –

for mirth and laziness
time to be human.

DORIS KAREVA
translated from the Estonian by Tiina Aleman

The Guest House

This being human is a guesthouse.
Every morning a new arrival.

A joy, a depression, a meanness,
some momentary awareness comes
as an unexpected visitor.

Welcome and entertain them all!
Even if they're a crowd of sorrows,
who violently sweep your house
empty of its furniture,
still, treat each guest honorably.
He may be clearing you out
for some new delight.

The dark thought, the shame, the malice,
meet them at the door laughing,
and invite them in.

Be grateful for whoever comes,
because each has been sent
as a guide from beyond.

RUMI
translated from the Persian by Coleman Barks with John Moyne

'To be great, be whole...'

To be great, be whole: don't exaggerate
            Or leave out any part of you.
Be complete in each thing. Put all you are
            Into the least of your acts.
So too in each lake, with its lofty life,
            The whole moon shines.

FERNANDO PESSOA
translated from the Portuguese by Richard Zenith

Living

The fire in leaf and grass
so green it seems
each summer the last summer.

The wind blowing, the leaves
shivering in the sun,
each day the last day.

A red salamander
so cold and so
easy to catch, dreamily

moves his delicate feet
and long tail. I hold
my hand open for him to go.

Each minute the last minute.

DENISE LEVERTOV

Table

A man filled with the gladness of living
Put his keys on the table,
Put flowers in a copper bowl there.
He put his eggs and milk on the table.
He put there the light that came in through the window,
Sound of a bicycle, sound of a spinning wheel.
The softness of bread and weather he put there.
On the table the man put
Things that happened in his mind.
What he wanted to do in life,
He put that there.
Those he loved, those he didn't love,
The man put them on the table too.
Three times three make nine:
The man put nine on the table.
He was next to the window next to the sky;
He reached out and placed on the table endlessness.
So many days he had wanted to drink a beer!
He put on the table the pouring of that beer.
He placed there his sleep and his wakefulness;
His hunger and his fullness he put there.

Now that's what I call a table!
It didn't complain at all about the load.
It wobbled once or twice, then stood firm.
The man kept piling things on.

EDIP CANSEVER
translated from the Turkish by
Julia Clare Tillinghast & Richard Tillinghast

Second-Hand Coat

I feel
in her pockets; she wore nice cotton gloves,
kept a handkerchief box, washed her undies,
ate at the Holiday Inn, had a basement freezer,
belonged to a bridge club.
I think when I wake in the morning
that I have turned into her.
She hangs in the hall downstairs,
a shadow with pulled threads.
I slip her over my arms, skin of a matron.
Where are you? I say to myself, to the orphaned body,
and her coat says,
Get your purse, have you got your keys?

RUTH STONE

Could Have

It could have happened.
It had to happen.
It happened earlier. Later.
Nearer. Farther off.
It happened, but not to you.

You were saved because you were the first.
You were saved because you were the last.
Alone. With others.
On the right. The left.
Because it was raining. Because of the shade.
Because the day was sunny.

You were in luck – there was a forest.
You were in luck – there were no trees.
You were in luck – a rake, a hook, a beam, a brake,
a jamb, a turn, a quarter-inch, an instant...
You were in luck – just then a straw went floating by.

As a result, because, although, despite.
What would have happened if a hand, a foot,
within an inch, a hairsbreadth from
an unfortunate coincidence.

So you're here? Still dizzy from another dodge, close shave, reprieve?
One hole in the net and you slipped through?
I couldn't be more shocked or speechless.
Listen,
how your heart pounds inside me.

WISŁAWA SZYMBORSKA
translated from the Polish by Stanislav Barańczak & Clare Cavanagh

Dawn Revisited

Imagine you wake up
with a second chance: The blue jay
hawks his pretty wares
and the oak still stands, spreading
glorious shade. If you don't look back,

the future never happens.
How good to rise in sunlight,
in the prodigal smell of biscuits –
eggs and sausage on the grill.
The whole sky is yours

to write on, blown open
to a blank page. Come on,
shake a leg! You'll never know
who's down there, frying those eggs,
if you don't get up and see.

RITA DOVE

The door

Go and open the door.
  Maybe outside there's
  a tree, or a wood,
  a garden,
  or a magic city.

Go and open the door.
  Maybe a dog's rummaging.
  Maybe you'll see a face,
or an eye,
or the picture
              of a picture.

Go and open the door.
  If there's a fog
  it will clear.

Go and open the door.
  Even if there's only
  the darkness ticking,
  even if there's only
  the hollow wind,
  even if
          nothing
                    is there,
go and open the door.

At least
there'll be
a draught.

MIROSLAV HOLUB
translated from the Czech by Ian Milner

Otherwise

I got out of bed
on two strong legs.
It might have been
otherwise. I ate
cereal, sweet
milk, ripe, flawless
peach. It might
have been otherwise.
I took the dog uphill
to the birchwood.
All morning I did
the work I love.

At noon I lay down
with my mate. It might
have been otherwise.
We ate dinner together
at a table with silver
candlesticks. It might
have been otherwise.
I slept in a bed
in a room with paintings
on the walls, and
planned another day
just like this day.
But one day, I know,
it will be otherwise.

JANE KENYON

Harlem [2]

What happens to a dream deferred?

    Does it dry up
    like a raisin in the sun?
    Or fester like a sore –
    And then run?
    Does it stink like rotten meat?
    Or crust and sugar over –
    like a syrupy sweet?

    Maybe it just sags
    like a heavy load.

    Or does it explode?

LANGSTON HUGHES

Archaic Torso of Apollo

We cannot know his legendary head
with eyes like ripening fruit. And yet his torso
is still suffused with brilliance from inside,
like a lamp, in which his gaze, now turned to low,

gleams in all its power. Otherwise
the curved breast could not dazzle you so, nor could
a smile run through the placid hips and thighs
to that dark center where procreation flared.

Otherwise this stone would seem defaced
beneath the translucent cascade of the shoulders
and would not glisten like a wild beast's fur:

would not, from all the borders of itself,
burst like a star: for here there is no place
that does not see you. You must change your life.

RAINER MARIA RILKE
translated from the German by Stephen Mitchell

The Journey

One day you finally knew
what you had to do, and began,
though the voices around you
kept shouting
their bad advice –

though the whole house
began to tremble
and you felt the old tug
at your ankles.
'Mend my life!'
each voice cried.
But you didn't stop.
You knew what you had to do,
though the wind pried
with its stiff fingers
at the very foundations,
though their melancholy
was terrible.
It was already late
enough, and a wild night,
and the road full of fallen
branches and stones.
But little by little,
as you left their voices behind,
the stars began to burn
through the sheets of clouds,
and there was a new voice,
which you slowly
recognised as your own,
that kept you company
as you strode deeper and deeper
into the world,
determined to do
the only thing you could do –
determined to save
the only life you could save.

MARY OLIVER

Lying in a Hammock at William Duffy's Farm in Pine Island, Minnesota

Over my head, I see the bronze butterfly,
Asleep on the black trunk,
Blowing like a leaf in green shadow.
Down the ravine behind the empty house,
The cowbells follow one another
Into the distances of the afternoon.
To my right,
In a field of sunlight between two pines,
The droppings of last year's horses
Blaze up into golden stones.
I lean back as the evening darkens and comes on.
A chicken hawk floats over, looking for home.
I have wasted my life.

JAMES WRIGHT

Temptation

Call yourself alive? Look, I promise you
that for the first time you'll feel your pores opening
like fish mouths, and you'll actually be able to hear
your blood surging through all those lanes,
and you'll feel light gliding across the cornea
like the train of a dress. For the first time
you'll be aware of gravity
like a thorn in your heel,
and your shoulder blades will ache for want of wings.
Call yourself alive? I promise you
you'll be deafened by dust falling on the furniture,
you'll feel your eyebrows turning to two gashes,
and every memory you have – will begin
at Genesis.

NINA CASSIAN
translated from the Romanian by Brenda Walker & Andrea Deletant

Begin

Begin again to the summoning birds
to the sight of light at the window,
begin to the roar of morning traffic
all along Pembroke Road.
Every beginning is a promise
born in light and dying in dark
determination and exaltation of springtime
flowering the way to work.
Begin to the pageant of queuing girls
the arrogant loneliness of swans in the canal
bridges linking the past and future
old friends passing though with us still.
Begin to the loneliness that cannot end
since it perhaps is what makes us begin,
begin to wonder at unknown faces
at crying birds in the sudden rain
at branches stark in the willing sunlight
at seagulls foraging for bread
at couples sharing a sunny secret
alone together while making good.
Though we live in a world that dreams of ending
that always seems about to give in
something that will not acknowledge conclusion
insists that we forever begin.

BRENDAN KENNELLY

As I Go

My pot is an old paint container
I do not know
who bought it
I do not know
whose house it decorated
I picked up the empty tin
in Cemetery Lane.
My lamp, a paraffin lamp
is an empty 280ml bottle
labelled 40 per cent alcohol
I picked up the bottle in a trash bin.
My cup
is an old jam tin
I do not know who enjoyed the sweetness
I found the tin
in a storm-water drain.
My plate is a motor car hub-cap cover
I do not know
whose car it belonged to
I found a boy wheeling it, playing with it
My house is built
from plastic over cardboard
I found the plastic being blown by the wind
It's simple
I pick up my life
as I go.

JULIUS CHINGONO

Ithaka

As you set out for Ithaka
hope your road is a long one,
full of adventure, full of discovery,
Laistrygonians, Cyclops,
angry Poseidon – don't be afraid of them:
you'll never find things like that on your way
as long as you keep your thoughts raised high,
as long as a rare excitement
stirs your spirit and your body.
Laistrygonians, Cyclops,
wild Poseidon – you won't encounter them
unless you bring them along inside your soul,
unless your soul sets them up in front of you.

Hope your road is a long one.
May there be many summer mornings when,
with what pleasure, what joy,
you enter harbours you're seeing for the first time;
may you stop at Phoenician trading stations
to buy fine things,
mother of pearl and coral, amber and ebony,
sensual perfume of every kind –
as many sensual perfumes as you can;
and may you visit many Egyptian cities
to learn and go on learning from their scholars.

Keep Ithaka always in your mind.
Arriving there is what you're destined for.
But don't hurry the journey at all.
Better if it lasts for years,
so you're old by the time you reach the island,
wealthy with all you've gained on the way,
not expecting Ithaka to make you rich.

Ithaka gave you the marvellous journey.
Without her you wouldn't have set out.
She has nothing left to give you now.

And if you find her poor, Ithaka won't have fooled you.
Wise as you will have become, so full of experience,
you'll have understood by then what these Ithakas mean.

C.P. CAVAFY
translated from the Greek by Edmund Keeley & Philip Sherrard

The Layers

I have walked through many lives,
some of them my own,
and I am not who I was,
though some principle of being
abides, from which I struggle
not to stray.
When I look behind,
as I am compelled to look
before I can gather strength
to proceed on my journey,
I see the milestones dwindling
toward the horizon
and the slow fires trailing
from the abandoned camp-sites,
over which scavenger angels
wheel on heavy wings.
Oh, I have made myself a tribe
out of my true affections,
and my tribe is scattered!

How shall the heart be reconciled
to its feast of losses?
In a rising wind
the manic dust of my friends,
those who fell along the way,
bitterly stings my face.
Yet I turn, I turn,
exulting somewhat,
with my will intact to go
wherever I need to go,
and every stone on the road
precious to me.
In my darkest night,
when the moon was covered
and I roamed through wreckage,
a nimbus-clouded voice
directed me:
'Live in the layers,
not on the litter.'
Though I lack the art
to decipher it,
no doubt the next chapter
in my book of transformations
is already written.
I am not done with my changes.

STANLEY KUNITZ

The Road Not Taken

Two roads diverged in a yellow wood,
And sorry I could not travel both
And be one traveler, long I stood
And looked down one as far as I could
To where it bent in the undergrowth;

Then took the other, as just as fair,
And having perhaps the better claim,
Because it was grassy and wanted wear;
Though as for that, the passing there
Had worn them really about the same,

And both that morning equally lay
In leaves no step had trodden black.
Oh, I kept the first for another day!
Yet knowing how way leads on to way,
I doubted if I should ever come back.

I shall be telling this with a sigh
Somewhere ages and ages hence:
Two roads diverged in a wood, and I –
I took the one less traveled by,
And that has made all the difference.

ROBERT FROST

The Way It Is

There's a thread you follow. It goes among
things that change. But it doesn't change.
People wonder about what you are pursuing.
You have to explain about the thread.
But it is hard for others to see.
While you hold it you can't get lost.
Tragedies happen; people get hurt
or die; and you suffer and get old.
Nothing you do can stop time's unfolding.
You don't ever let go of the thread.

WILLIAM STAFFORD

'I drew a line...'

I drew a line:
this far, and no further,
never will I go further than this.

When I went further,
I drew a new line,
and then another line.

The sun was shining
and everywhere I saw people,
hurried and serious,
and everyone was drawing a line,
everyone went further.

TOON TELLEGEN
translated from the Dutch by Judith Wilkinson

Stopping by Woods on a Snowy Evening

Whose woods these are I think I know.
His house is in the village, though;
He will not see me stopping here
To watch his woods fill up with snow.

My little horse must think it queer
To stop without a farmhouse near
Between the woods and frozen lake
The darkest evening of the year.

He gives his harness bells a shake
To ask if there is some mistake.
The only other sound's the sweep
Of easy wind and downy flake.

The woods are lovely, dark and deep,
But I have promises to keep,
And miles to go before I sleep,
And miles to go before I sleep.

ROBERT FROST

Migratory

Near evening, in Fairhaven, Massachusetts,
seventeen wild geese arrowed the ashen blue
over the Wal-Mart and the Blockbuster Video,

and I was up there, somewhere between the asphalt
and their clear dominion – not in the parking lot,
its tallowy circles just appearing,

the shopping carts shining, from above,
like little scraps of foil. Their eyes
held me there, the unfailing gaze

of those who know how to fly in formation,
wing-tip to wing-tip, safe, fearless.
And the convex glamour of their eyes carried

the parking lot, the wet field
troubled with muffler shops
and stoplights, the arc of highway

and its exits, one shattered farmhouse
with its failing barn... The wind
a few hundred feet above the grass

erases the mechanical noises, everything;
nothing but their breathing
and the perfect rowing of the pinions,

and then, out of that long, percussive pour
toward what they are most certain of,
comes their – question, is it?

Assertion, prayer, aria – as delivered
by something too compelled in its passage
to sing? A hoarse and unwieldy music

which plays nonetheless down the length
of me until I am involved in their flight,
the unyielding necessity of it, as they literally

rise above, ineluctable, heedless,
needing nothing... Only animals
make me believe in God now

– so little between spirit and skin,
any gesture so entirely themselves.
But I wasn't with them,

as they headed toward Acushnet
and New Bedford, of course I wasn't,
though I was not exactly in the parking lot

either, where the cars nudged in and out
of their slots, each taking the place another
had abandoned, so that no space, no desire

would remain unfilled. I wasn't there.
I was so filled with longing
– is that what that sound is for? –

I seemed to be nowhere at all.

MARK DOTY

Alone

I

One evening in February I came near to dying here.
The car skidded sideways on the ice, out
on the wrong side of the road. The approaching cars –
their lights – closed in.

My name, my girls, my job
broke free and were left silently behind
further and further away. I was anonymous
like a boy in a playground surrounded by enemies.

The approaching traffic had huge lights.
They shone on me while I pulled at the wheel
in a transparent terror that floated like egg white.
The seconds grew – there was space in them –
they grew as big as hospital buildings.

You could almost pause
and breathe out for a while
before being crushed.

Then something caught: a helping grain of sand
or a wonderful gust of wind. The car broke free
and scuttled smartly right over the road.
A post shot up and cracked – a sharp clang – it
flew away in the darkness.

Then – stillness. I sat back in my seat-belt
and saw someone coming through the whirling snow
to see what had become of me.

II

I have been walking for a long time
on the frozen Östergötland fields.
I have not seen a single person.

In other parts of the world
there are people who are born, live and die
in a perpetual crowd.

To be always visible – to live
in a swarm of eyes –
a special expression must develop.
Face coated with clay.

The murmuring rises and falls
while they divide up among themselves
the sky, the shadows, the sand grains.

I must be alone
ten minutes in the morning
and ten minutes in the evening.
– Without a programme.

Everyone is queuing at everyone's door.

Many.

One.

TOMAS TRANSTRÖMER
translated from the Swedish by Robin Fulton

Encounter

We were riding through frozen fields in a wagon at dawn.
A red wing rose in the darkness.

And suddenly a hare ran across the road.
One of us pointed to it with his hand.

That was long ago. Today neither of them is alive,
Not the hare, nor the man who made the gesture.

O my love, where are they, where are they going
The flash of a hand, streak of movement, rustle of pebbles.
I ask not out of sorrow, but in wonder.

CZESŁAW MIŁOSZ
translated by Czesław Miłosz & Lillian Vallee

At the Fishhouses

Although it is a cold evening,
down by one of the fishhouses
an old man sits netting,
his net, in the gloaming almost invisible,
a dark purple-brown,
and his shuttle worn and polished.
The air smells so strong of codfish
it makes one's nose run and one's eyes water.
The five fishhouses have steeply peaked roofs
and narrow, cleated gangplanks slant up
to storerooms in the gables
for the wheelbarrows to be pushed up and down on.
All is silver: the heavy surface of the sea,
swelling slowly as if considering spilling over,

is opaque, but the silver of the benches,
the lobster pots, and masts, scattered
among the wild jagged rocks,
is of an apparent translucence
like the small old buildings with an emerald moss
growing on their shoreward walls.
The big fish tubs are completely lined
with layers of beautiful herring scales
and the wheelbarrows are similarly plastered
with creamy iridescent coats of mail,
with small iridescent flies crawling on them.
Up on the little slope behind the houses,
set in the sparse bright sprinkle of grass,
is an ancient wooden capstan,
cracked, with two long bleached handles
and some melancholy stains, like dried blood,
where the ironwork has rusted.
The old man accepts a Lucky Strike.
He was a friend of my grandfather.
We talk of the decline in the population
and of codfish and herring
while he waits for a herring boat to come in.
There are sequins on his vest and on his thumb.
He has scraped the scales, the principal beauty,
from unnumbered fish with that black old knife,
the blade of which is almost worn away.

Down at the water's edge, at the place
where they haul up the boats, up the long ramp
descending into the water, thin silver
tree trunks are laid horizontally
across the gray stones, down and down
at intervals of four or five feet.

Cold dark deep and absolutely clear,
element bearable to no mortal,
to fish and to seals... One seal particularly
I have seen here evening after evening.

He was curious about me. He was interested in music;
like me a believer in total immersion,
so I used to sing him Baptist hymns.
I also sang 'A Mighty Fortress Is Our God'.
He stood up in the water and regarded me
steadily, moving his head a little.
Then he would disappear, then suddenly emerge
almost in the same spot, with a sort of shrug
as if it were against his better judgment.
Cold dark deep and absolutely clear,
the clear gray icy water... Back, behind us,
the dignified tall firs begin.
Bluish, associating with their shadows,
a million Christmas trees stand
waiting for Christmas. The water seems suspended
above the rounded gray and blue-gray stones.
I have seen it over and over, the same sea, the same,
slightly, indifferently swinging above the stones,
icily free above the stones,
above the stones and then the world.
If you should dip your hand in,
your wrist would ache immediately,
your bones would begin to ache and your hand would burn
as if the water were a transmutation of fire
that feeds on stones and burns with a dark gray flame.
If you tasted it, it would first taste bitter,
then briny, then surely burn your tongue.
It is like what we imagine knowledge to be:
dark, salt, clear, moving, utterly free,
drawn from the cold hard mouth
of the world, derived from the rocky breasts
forever, flowing and drawn, and since
our knowledge is historical, flowing, and flown.

ELIZABETH BISHOP

Snow

The room was suddenly rich and the great bay-window was
Spawning snow and pink roses against it
Soundlessly collateral and incompatible:
World is suddener than we fancy it.

World is crazier and more of it than we think,
Incorrigibly plural. I peel and portion
A tangerine and spit the pips and feel
The drunkenness of things being various.

And the fire flames with a bubbling sound for world
Is more spiteful and gay than one supposes –
On the tongue on the eyes on the ears in the palms of one's hands –
There is more than glass between the snow and the huge roses.

LOUIS MACNEICE

A Disused Shed in Co. Wexford

Let them not forget us, the weak souls among the asphodels.
SEFERIS, Mythistorema

(for J.G. Farrell)

Even now there are places where a thought might grow —
Peruvian mines, worked out and abandoned
To a slow clock of condensation,
An echo trapped for ever, and a flutter
Of wild flowers in the lift-shaft,
Indian compounds where the wind dances
And a door bangs with diminished confidence,
Lime crevices behind rippling rain-barrels,
Dog corners for bone burials;
And in a disused shed in Co. Wexford,

Deep in the grounds of a burnt-out hotel,
Among the bathtubs and the washbasins
A thousand mushrooms crowd to a keyhole.
This is the one star in their firmament
Or frames a star within a star.
What should they do there but desire?
So many days beyond the rhododendrons
With the world waltzing in its bowl of cloud,
They have learnt patience and silence
Listening to the rooks querulous in the high wood.

They have been waiting for us in a foetor
Of vegetable sweat since civil war days,
Since the gravel-crunching, interminable departure
Of the expropriated mycologist.
He never came back, and light since then
Is a keyhole rusting gently after rain.
Spiders have spun, flies dusted to mildew
And once a day, perhaps, they have heard something —
A trickle of masonry, a shout from the blue
Or a lorry changing gear at the end of the lane.

There have been deaths, the pale flesh flaking
Into the earth that nourished it;
And nightmares, born of these and the grim
Dominion of stale air and rank moisture.
Those nearest the door grow strong –
'Elbow room! Elbow room!'
The rest, dim in a twilight of crumbling
Utensils and broken pitchers, groaning
For their deliverance, have been so long
Expectant that there is left only the posture.

A half century, without visitors, in the dark –
Poor preparation for the cracking lock
And creak of hinges; magi, moonmen,
Powdery prisoners of the old regime,
Web-throated, stalked like triffids, racked by drought
And insomnia, only the ghost of a scream
At the flash-bulb firing-squad we wake them with
Shows there is life yet in their feverish forms.
Grown beyond nature now, soft food for worms,
They lift frail heads in gravity and good faith.

They are begging us, you see, in their wordless way,
To do something, to speak on their behalf
Or at least not to close the door again.
Lost people of Treblinka and Pompeii!
'Save us, save us,' they seem to say,
'Let the god not abandon us
Who have come so far in darkness and in pain.
We too had our lives to live.
You with your light meter and relaxed itinerary,
Let not our naive labours have been in vain!'

DEREK MAHON

Unwittingly

I've visited the place
where thought begins:
pear trees suspended in sunlight, narrow shops,
alleys to nothing

but nettles
and broken wars;
and though it might look different
to you:

a seaside town, with steep roofs
the colour of oysters,
the corner of some junkyard with its glint
of coming rain,

though someone else again would recognise
the warm barn, the smell of milk,
the wintered cattle
shifting in the dark,

it's always the same lit space,
the one good measure:
Sometimes you'll wake in a chair
as the light is fading,

or stop on the way to work
as a current of starlings
turns on itself
and settles above the green,

and because what we learn in the dark
remains all our lives,
a noise like the sea, displacing the day's
pale knowledge,

you'll come to yourself
in a glimmer of rainfall or frost,
the burnt smell of autumn,
a meeting of parallel lines,

and know you were someone else
for the longest time,
pretending you knew where you were, like a diffident tourist,
lost on the one main square, and afraid to enquire.

JOHN BURNSIDE

The Girl

One day life stands
gently smiling like a girl
suddenly on the far side of the stream
and asks
(in her annoying way),

But how did you end up there?

LARS GUSTAFSSON
translated from the Swedish by John Irons

Being the third song of Urias

Lives ago, years past generations
perhaps nowhere I dreamed it:
the foggy ploughland of wind
and hoofprints, my father
off in the mist topping beets.

Where I was eight, I knew nothing,
the world a cold winter light
on half a dozen fields, then
all the winking blether of stars.

Before like a fool I began
explaining the key in its lost locked box
adding words to the words to the sum
that never works out.

                    Where I was
distracted again by the lapwing,
the damp morning air of my father's
gregarious plainchant cursing
all that his masters deserved
and had paid for.
                    Sure I was
then for the world's mere being
in the white rime on weeds
among the wet hawthorn berries
at the field's edge darkened by frost,
and none of these damned words to say it.

I began trailing out there in voices,
friends, women, my children,
my father's tetherless anger, some
like him who are dead who are
part of the rain now.

KEN SMITH

46

Starlight

My father stands in the warm evening
on the porch of my first house.
I am four years old and growing tired.
I see his head among the stars,
the glow of his cigarette, redder
than the summer moon riding
low over the old neighborhood. We
are alone, and he asks me if I am happy.
'Are you happy?' I cannot answer.
I do not really understand the word,
and the voice, my father's voice, is not
his voice, but somehow thick and choked,
a voice I have not heard before, but
heard often since. He bends and passes
a thumb beneath each of my eyes.
The cigarette is gone, but I can smell
the tiredness that hangs on his breath.
He has found nothing, and he smiles
and holds my head with both his hands.
Then he lifts me to his shoulder,
and now I too am there among the stars
as tall as he. Are you happy? I say.
He nods in answer, Yes! oh yes! oh yes!
And in that new voice he says nothing
holding my head tight against his head,
his eyes closed up against the starlight,
as though those tiny blinking eyes
of light might find a tall, gaunt child
holding his child against the promises
of autumn, until the boy slept
never to waken in that world again.

PHILIP LEVINE

from Clearances

(in memoriam M.K.H., 1911-1984)

When all the others were away at Mass
I was all hers as we peeled potatoes.
They broke the silence, let fall one by one
Like solder weeping off the soldering iron:
Cold comforts set between us, things to share
Gleaming in a bucket of clean water.
And again let fall. Little pleasant splashes
From each other's work would bring us to our senses.

So while the parish priest at her bedside
Went hammer and tongs at the prayers for the dying
And some were responding and some crying
I remembered her head bent towards my head,
Her breath in mine, our fluent dipping knives –
Never closer the whole rest of our lives.

SEAMUS HEANEY

Poem for a Daughter

'I think I'm going to have it,'
I said, joking between pains.
The midwife rolled competent
sleeves over corpulent milky arms.
'Dear, you never have it,
we deliver it.'
A judgement years proved true.
Certainly I've never had you

as you still have me, Caroline.
Why does a mother need a daughter?
Heart's needle, hostage to fortune,
freedom's end. Yet nothing's more perfect
than that bleating, razor-shaped cry
that delivers a mother to her baby.
The bloodcord snaps that held
their sphere together. The child,
tiny and alone, creates the mother.

A woman's life is her own
until it is taken away
by a first particular cry.
Then she is not alone
but part of the premises
of everything there is:
a time, a tribe, a war.
When we belong to the world
we become what we are.

ANNE STEVENSON

Love

I hadn't met his kind before.
His misericord face – really
like a joke on his father – blurred
as if from years of polish;
his hands like curled dry leaves;

the profligate heat he gave
out, gave out, his shallow,
careful breaths: I thought
his filaments would blow,
I thought he was an emperor,

dying on silk cushions.
I didn't know how to keep
him wrapped, I didn't know
how to give him suck, I had
no idea about him. At night

I tried to remember the feel
of his head on my neck, the skull
small as a cat's, the soft spot
hot as a smelted coin,
and the hair, the down, fine

as the innermost, vellum layer
of some rare snowcreature's
aureole of fur, if you could meet
such a beast, if you could
get so near. I started there.

KATE CLANCHY

The Victory

I thought you were my victory
though you cut me like a knife
when I brought you out of my body
into your life.

Tiny antagonist, gory,
blue as a bruise. The stains
of your cloud of glory
bled from my veins.

How can you dare, blind thing,
blank insect eyes?
You barb the air. You sting
with bladed cries.

Snail. Scary knot of desires.
Hungry snarl. Small son.
Why do I have to love you?
How have you won?

ANNE STEVENSON

She Leaves Me

She betrays me, she leaves me.
She pushes me out of herself, and leaves me.
She offers herself to feed on, and leaves me.
She rocks me and she leaves me.
Wipes my bottom, combs my hair,
caresses the soles of my feet, but leaves me.
My nose drinks in her fragrance, how she hugs me:
she says, 'I'll never leave you!' And she leaves me.
She tricks me: smiling, whispers 'Don't be scared!'
I *am* scared, and I'm cold, and yet she leaves me.
She lies down on the bed with me at evening,
but soon enough she slips away and leaves me.
She is so big, so warm, alive, a nest,
she kisses me, and hums to me, and leaves me.
She presses sweets into my open palms
and 'There you are, eat now,' she says, and leaves me.
I cry and howl and press her frame to mine;
I can hold her, hit her too; and yet she leaves me.
She shuts the door, does not look back at all,
I'm nothing when she leaves me.
I wait for her return, a cringing cur:
she then arrives and strokes me, and she leaves me.
I need her – it is death to live without her –
she picks me up to warm me, and she leaves me.
Her arms make up a cage, her lap's a house;
I'd love to go back in there, but she leaves me.
I come to one conclusion: I'm not her:
a stranger, she's a stranger, and she leaves me.

Out there's the world, where someone will be waiting!
For you, there will be someone there to leave.
Don't look back. Shut the door. You know
how easy it is to wait, how hard to go.

Some you'll grieve, others will deceive you,
some will wait, others fear your lack,
and some there'll always be who don't come back:
they give you life, but then they die and leave you.

ANNA T. SZABÓ
translated from the Hungarian by Clive Wilmer & George Gömöri

A Little Tooth

Your baby grows a tooth, then two,
and four, and five, then she wants some meat
directly from the bone. It's all

over: she'll learn some words, she'll fall
in love with cretins, dolts, a sweet
talker on his way to jail. And you,

your wife, get old, flyblown, and rue
nothing. You did, you loved, your feet
are sore. It's dusk. Your daughter's tall.

THOMAS LUX

After Making Love We Hear Footsteps

For I can snore like a bullhorn
or play loud music
or sit up talking with any reasonably sober Irishman
and Fergus will only sink deeper
into his dreamless sleep, which goes by all in one flash,
but let there be that heavy breathing
or a stifled come-cry anywhere in the house
and he will wrench himself awake
and make for it on the run – as now, we lie together,
after making love, quiet, touching along the length of our bodies,
familiar touch of the long-married,
and he appears – in his baseball pajamas, it happens,
the neck opening so small he has to screw them on –
and flops down between us and hugs us and snuggles himself to
            sleep,
his face gleaming with satisfaction at being this very child.

In the half darkness we look at each other
and smile
and touch arms across this little, startlingly muscled body –
this one whom habit of memory propels to the ground of his
            making,
sleeper only the mortal sounds can sing awake,
this blessing love gives again into our arms.

GALWAY KINNELL

54

Great Things Have Happened

We were talking about the great things
that have happened in our lifetimes;
and I said, 'Oh, I suppose the moon landing
was the greatest thing that has happened
in my time.' But, of course, we were all lying.
The truth is the moon landing didn't mean
one-tenth as much to me as one night in 1963
when we lived in a three-room flat in what once had been
the mansion of some Victorian merchant prince
(our kitchen had been a clothes closet, I'm sure),
on a street where by now nobody lived
who could afford to live anywhere else.
That night, the three of us, Claudine, Johnnie and me,
woke up at half-past four in the morning
and ate cinnamon toast together.

'Is that all?' I hear somebody ask.

Oh, but we were silly with sleepiness
and, under our windows, the street-cleaners
were working their machines and conversing in Italian, and
everything was strange without being threatening,
even the tea-kettle whistled differently
than in the daytime: it was like the feeling
you get sometimes in a country you've never visited
before, when the bread doesn't taste quite the same,
the butter is a small adventure, and they put
paprika on the table instead of pepper,
except that there was nobody in this country
except the three of us, half-tipsy with the wonder
of being alive, and wholly enveloped in love.

ALDEN NOWLAN

This Hour

We could never really say what it is like,
this hour of drinking wine together
on a hot summer night, in the living-room
with the windows open, in our underwear,
my pants with pale-gold gibbon monkeys on them
gleaming in the heat. We talk about our son disap-
pearing between the pine boughs,
we could not tell what was chrysalis or
bough and what was him. The wine
is powerful, each mouthful holds
for a moment its amber agate shape,
I think of the sweat I sipped from my father's
forehead the hour before his death. We talk about
those last days – that I was waiting for him to die.
You are lying on the couch, your underpants
a luminous white, your hand resting
relaxed, alongside your penis,
we talk about your father's illness,
your nipple like a pure circle of
something risen to the surface of your chest.
Even if we wanted to,
we could not describe it,
the end of the second glass when I sometimes
weep and you start to get sleepy – I love
to drink and cry with you, and end up
sobbing to a sleeping man, your
long body filling the couch and
draped slightly over the ends, the
untrained soft singing of your snore, it cannot be given.
Yes, we know we will make love, but we're
not getting ready to make love,
nor are we getting over making love,
love is simply our element,
it is the summer night, we are in it.

SHARON OLDS

Snow Melting

Snow melting when I left you, and I took
This fragile bone we'd found in melting snow
Before I left, exposed beside a brook
Where raccoons washed their hands. And this, I know,

Is that raccoon we'd watched for every day.
Though at the time her wild human hand
Had gestured inexplicably, I say
Her meaning now is more than I can stand.

We've reasons, we have reasons, so we say,
For giving love, and for withholding it.
I who would love must marvel at the way
I know aloneness when I'm holding it,

Know near and far as words for live and die,
Know distance, as I'm trying to draw near,
Growing immense, and know, but don't know why,
Things seen up close enlarge, then disappear.

Tonight this small room seems too huge to cross.
And my life is that looming kind of place.
Here, left with this alone, and at a loss
I hold an alien and vacant face

Which shrinks away, and yet is magnified –
More so than I seem able to explain.
Tonight the giant galaxies outside
Are tiny, tiny on my windowpane.

GJERTRUD SCHNACKENBERG

Wild strawberries

What I get I bring home to you:
a dark handful, sweet-edged,
dissolving in one mouthful.

I bother to bring them for you
though they're so quickly over,
pulpless, sliding to juice,

a grainy rub on the tongue
and the taste's gone. If you remember
we were in the woods at wild strawberry time

and I was making a basket of dockleaves
to hold what you'd picked,
but the cold leaves unplaited themselves

and slid apart, and again unplaited themselves
until I gave up and ate wild strawberries
out of your hands for sweetness.

I lipped at your palm –
the little salt edge there,
the tang of money you'd handled.

As we stayed in the wood, hidden,
we heard the sound system below us
calling the winners at Chepstow,
faint as the breeze turned.

The sun came out on us, the shade blotches
went hazel: we heard names
bubble like stock-doves over the woods

as jockeys in stained silks gentled
those sweat-dark, shuddering horses
down to the walk.

HELEN DUNMORE

Strawberries

There were never strawberries
like the ones we had
that sultry afternoon
sitting on the step
of the open french window
facing each other
your knees held in mine
the blue plates in our laps
the strawberries glistening
in the hot sunlight
we dipped them in sugar
looking at each other
not hurrying the feast
for one to come
the empty plates
laid on the stone together
with the two forks crossed
and I bent towards you
sweet in that air
in my arms
abandoned like a child
from your eager mouth
the taste of strawberries
in my memory
lean back again
let me love you

let the sun beat
on our forgetfulness
one hour of all
the heat intense
and summer lightning
on the Kilpatrick hills

let the storm wash the plates

EDWIN MORGAN

For Desire

Give me the strongest cheese, the one that stinks best;
and I want the good wine, the swirl in crystal
surrendering the bruised scent of blackberries,
or cherries, the rich spurt in the back
of the throat, the holding it there before swallowing.
Give me the lover who yanks open the door
of his house and presses me to the wall
in the dim hallway, and keeps me there until I'm drenched
and shaking, whose kisses arrive by the boatload
and begin their delicious diaspora
through the cities and small towns of my body.
To hell with the saints, with the martyrs
of my childhood meant to instruct me
in the power of endurance and faith,
to hell with the next world and its pallid angels
swooning and sighing like Victorian girls.
I want this world. I want to walk into
the ocean and feel it trying to drag me along
like I'm nothing but a broken bit of scratched glass,
and I want to resist it. I want to go
staggering and flailing my way
through the bars and back rooms,
through the gleaming hotels and the weedy
lots of abandoned sunflowers and the parks
where dogs are let off their leashes
in spite of the signs, where they sniff each
other and roll together in the grass, I want to
lie down somewhere and suffer for love until
it nearly kills me, and then I want to get up again
and put on that little black dress and wait
for you, yes you, to come over here
and get down on your knees and tell me
just how fucking good I look.

KIM ADDONIZIO

You Don't Know What Love Is

but you know how to raise it in me
like a dead girl winched up from a river. How to
wash off the sludge, the stench of our past.
How to start clean. This love even sits up
and blinks; amazed, she takes a few shaky steps.
Any day now she'll try to eat solid food. She'll want
to get into a fast car, one low to the ground, and drive
to some cinderblock shithole in the desert
where she can drink and get sick and then
dance in nothing but her underwear. You know
where she's headed, you know she'll wake up
with an ache she can't locate and no money
and a terrible thirst. So to hell
with your warm hands sliding inside my shirt
and your tongue down my throat
like an oxygen tube. Cover me
in black plastic. Let the mourners through.

KIM ADDONIZIO

Atlas

There is a kind of love called maintenance,
Which stores the WD40 and knows when to use it;

Which checks the insurance, and doesn't forget
The milkman; which remembers to plant bulbs;

Which answers letters; which knows the way
The money goes; which deals with dentists

And Road Fund Tax and meeting trains,
And postcards to the lonely; which upholds

The permanently ricketty elaborate
Structures of living; which is Atlas.

And maintenance is the sensible side of love,
Which knows what time and weather are doing
To my brickwork; insulates my faulty wiring;
Laughs at my dryrotten jokes; remembers
My need for gloss and grouting; which keeps
My suspect edifice upright in air,
As Atlas did the sky.

U.A. FANTHORPE

Love Song: I and Thou

Nothing is plumb, level, or square:
   the studs are bowed, the joists
are shaky by nature, no piece fits
   any other piece without a gap
or pinch, and bent nails
   dance all over the surfacing
like maggots. By Christ
   I am no carpenter. I built
the roof for myself, the walls
   for myself, the floors
for myself, and got
   hung up in it myself. I
danced with a purple thumb
   at this house-warming, drunk
with my prime whiskey: rage.
   Oh I spat rage's nails
into the frame-up of my work:
   it held. It settled plumb,
level, solid, square and true
   for that great moment. Then
it screamed and went on through,
   skewing as wrong the other way.
God damned it. This is hell,
   but I planned it, I sawed it,
I nailed it, and I
   will live in it until it kills me.
I can nail my left palm
   to the left-hand crosspiece but
I can't do everything myself.
   I need a hand to nail the right,
a help, a love, a you, a wife.

ALAN DUGAN

Wedding

From time to time our love is like a sail
and when the sail begins to alternate
from tack to tack, it's like a swallowtail
and when the swallow flies it's like a coat;
and if the coat is yours, it has a tear
like a wide mouth and when the mouth begins
to draw the wind, it's like a trumpeter
and when the trumpet blows, it blows like millions
and this, my love, when millions come and go
beyond the need of us, is like a trick;
and when the trick begins, it's like a toe
tiptoeing on a rope, which is like luck;
and when the luck begins, it's like a wedding,
which is like love, which is like everything.

ALICE OSWALD

An Arundel Tomb

Side by side, their faces blurred,
The earl and countess lie in stone,
Their proper habits vaguely shown
As jointed armour, stiffened pleat,
And that faint hint of the absurd –
The little dogs under their feet.

Such plainness of the pre-baroque
Hardly involves the eye, until
It meets his left-hand gauntlet, still
Clasped empty in the other; and
One sees, with a sharp tender shock,
His hand withdrawn, holding her hand.

They would not think to lie so long.
Such faithfulness in effigy
Was just a detail friends would see:
A sculptor's sweet commissioned grace
Thrown off in helping to prolong
The Latin names around the base.

They would not guess how early in
Their supine stationary voyage
The air would change to soundless damage,
Turn the old tenantry away;
How soon succeeding eyes begin
To look, not read. Rigidly they

Persisted, linked, through lengths and breadths
Of time. Snow fell, undated. Light
Each summer thronged the glass. A bright
Litter of birdcalls strewed the same
Bone-riddled ground. And up the paths
The endless altered people came,

Washing at their identity.
Now, helpless in the hollow of
An unarmorial age, a trough
Of smoke in slow suspended skeins
Above their scrap of history,
Only an attitude remains:

Time has transfigured them into
Untruth. The stone fidelity
They hardly meant has come to be
Their final blazon, and to prove
Our almost-instinct almost true:
What will survive of us is love.

PHILIP LARKIN

Love after Love

The time will come
when, with elation,
you will greet yourself arriving
at your own door, in your own mirror
and each will smile at the other's welcome,

and say, sit here. Eat.
You will love again the stranger who was your self.
Give wine. Give bread, Give back your heart
to itself, to the stranger who has loved you

all your life, whom you ignored
for another, who knows you by heart.
Take down the love letters from the bookshelf,

the photographs, the desperate notes,
peel your own image from the mirror.
Sit. Feast on your life.

DEREK WALCOTT

Missing God

His grace is no longer called for
before meals: farmed fish multiply
without His intercession.
Bread production rises through
disease-resistant grains devised
scientifically to mitigate His faults.

Yet, though we rebelled against Him
like adolescents, uplifted to see
an oppressive father banished –
a bearded hermit – to the desert,
we confess to missing Him at times.

Miss Him during the civil wedding
when, at the blossomy altar
of the registrar's desk, we wait in vain
to be fed a line containing words
like 'everlasting' and 'divine'.

Miss Him when the TV scientist
explains the cosmos through equations,
leaving our planet to revolve on its axis
aimlessly, a wheel skidding in snow.

Miss Him when the radio catches a snatch
of plainchant from some echoey priory;
when the gospel choir raises its collective voice
to ask *Shall We Gather at the River?*
or the forces of the oratorio converge
on *I Know That My Redeemer Liveth*
and our contracted hearts lose a beat.

Miss Him when a choked voice at
the crematorium recites the poem
about fearing no more the heat of the sun.

Miss Him when we stand in judgement
on a lank Crucifixion in an art museum,
its stripe-like ribs testifying to rank.

Miss Him when the gamma-rays
recorded on the satellite graph
seem arranged into a celestial score,
the music of the spheres,
the *Ave Verum Corpus* of the observatory lab.

Miss Him when we stumble on the breast lump
for the first time and an involuntary prayer
escapes our lips; when a shadow crosses
our bodies on an x-ray screen; when we receive
a transfusion of foaming blood
sacrificed anonymously to save life.

Miss Him when we exclaim His name
spontaneously in awe or anger
as a woman in the birth ward
calls to her long-dead mother.

Miss Him when the linen-covered
dining-table holds warm bread rolls,
shiny glasses of red wine.

Miss Him when a dove swoops
from the orange grove in a tourist village
just as the monastery bell begins to take its toll.

Miss Him when our journey leads us
under leaves of Gothic tracery, an arch
of overlapping branches that meet
like hands in Michelangelo's *Creation*.

Miss Him when, trudging past a church,
we catch a residual blast of incense,
a perfume on par with the fresh-baked loaf
which Miłosz compared to happiness.

Miss Him when our newly-fitted kitchen
comes in Shaker-style and we order
a matching set of Mother Ann Lee chairs.

Miss Him when we listen to the prophecy
of astronomers that the visible galaxies
will recede as the universe expands.

Miss Him when the sunset makes
its presence felt in the stained glass
window of the fake antique lounge bar.

Miss Him the way an uncoupled glider
riding the evening thermals misses its tug.

Miss Him, as the lovers shrugging
shoulders outside the cheap hotel
ponder what their next move should be.

Even feel nostalgic, odd days,
for His Second Coming,
like standing in the brick
dome of a dovecote
after the birds have flown.

DENNIS O'DRISCOLL

Sheep Fair Day

*The real aim is not to see God in all things, it is that God,
through us, should see the things that we see.*
SIMONE WEIL

I took God with me to the sheep fair. I said, 'Look
there's Liv, sitting on the wall, waiting;
these are pens, these are sheep,
this is their shit we are walking in, this is their fear.
See that man over there, stepping along the low walls
between pens, eyes always watching,
mouth always talking, he is the auctioneer.
That is wind in the ash trees above, that is sun
splashing us with running light and dark.
Those men over there, the ones with their faces sealed,
are buying or selling. Beyond in the ring
where the beasts pour in, huddle and rush,
the hoggets are auctioned in lots.
And that woman with the ruddy face and the home-cut hair
and a new child on her arm, that is how it is to be woman
with the milk running, sitting on wooden boards
in this shit-milky place of animals and birth and death
as the bidding rises and falls.'

Then I went back outside and found Fintan.
I showed God his hand as he sat on the rails,
how he let it trail down and his fingers played
in the curly back of a ewe. Fintan's a sheep-man
he's deep into sheep, though it's cattle he keeps now,
for sound commercial reasons.
                              'Feel that,' I said,
'feel with my heart the force in that hand
that's twining her wool as he talks.'
Then I went with Fintan and Liv to Refreshments,
I let God sip tea, boiling hot, from a cup,
and I lent God my fingers to feel how they burned
when I tripped on a stone and it slopped.
'This is hurt,' I said, 'there'll be more.'

And the morning wore on and the sun climbed
and God felt how it is when I stand too long,
how the sickness rises, how the muscles burn.

Later, at the back end of the afternoon,
I went down to swim in the green slide of river,
I worked my way under the bridge, against the current,
then I showed how it is to turn onto your back
with, above you and a long way up, two gossiping pigeons,
and a clump of valerian, holding itself to the sky.
I remarked on the stone arch as I drifted through it,
how it dapples with sunlight from the water,
how the bridge hunkers down, crouching low in its track
and roars when a lorry drives over.

And later again, in the kitchen,
wrung out, at day's ending, and empty,
I showed how it feels
to undo yourself,
to dissolve, and grow age-old, nameless:

woman sweeping a floor, darkness growing.

KERRY HARDIE

from Of Gravity and Light
(enlightenment)

What we need most, we learn from the menial tasks:
the novice raking sand in Buddhist texts,
or sweeping leaves, his hands chilled to the bone,
while understanding hovers out of reach;
the changeling in a folk tale, chopping logs,
poised at the dizzy edge of transformation;

and everything they do is gravity:
swaying above the darkness of the well
to haul the bucket in; guiding the broom;
finding the body's kinship with the earth
beneath their feet, the lattice of a world
where nothing turns or stands outside the whole;

and when the insight comes, they carry on
with what's at hand: the gravel path; the fire;
knowing the soul is no more difficult
than water, or the fig tree by the well
that stood for decades, barren and inert,
till every branch was answered in the stars.

JOHN BURNSIDE

The Bright Field

I have seen the sun break through
to illuminate a small field
for a while, and gone my way
and forgotten it. But that was the pearl
of great price, the one field that had
the treasure in it. I realise now
that I must give all that I have
to possess it. Life is not hurrying

on to a receding future, nor hankering after
an imagined past. It is the turning
aside like Moses to the miracle
of the lit bush, to a brightness
that seemed as transitory as your youth
once, but is the eternity that awaits you.

R.S. THOMAS

Stationery

The moon did not become the sun.
It just fell on the desert
in great sheets, reams
of silver handmade by you.
The night is your cottage industry now,
the day is your brisk emporium.
The world is full of paper.

Write to me.

AGHA SHAHID ALI

The Love Song of J. Alfred Prufrock

S'io credessi che mia risposta fosse
a persona che mai tornasse al mondo,
questa fiamma staria senza più scosse.
Ma per ciò che giammai di questo fondo
non tornò vivo alcun, s'i'odo il vero,
senza tema d'infamia ti rispondo.

Let us go then, you and I,
When the evening is spread out against the sky
Like a patient etherised upon a table;
Let us go, through certain half-deserted streets,
The muttering retreats
Of restless nights in one-night cheap hotels
And sawdust restaurants with oyster-shells:
Streets that follow like a tedious argument
Of insidious intent
To lead you to an overwhelming question...
Oh, do not ask, 'What is it?'
Let us go and make our visit.

In the room the women come and go
Talking of Michelangelo.

The yellow fog that rubs its back upon the window-panes,
The yellow smoke that rubs its muzzle on the window-panes,
Licked its tongue into the corners of the evening,
Lingered upon the pools that stand in drains,
Let fall upon its back the soot that falls from chimneys,
Slipped by the terrace, made a sudden leap,
And seeing that it was a soft October night,
Curled once about the house, and fell asleep.

And indeed there will be time
For the yellow smoke that slides along the street
Rubbing its back upon the window-panes;
There will be time, there will be time
To prepare a face to meet the faces that you meet;

There will be time to murder and create,
And time for all the works and days of hands
That lift and drop a question on your plate;
Time for you and time for me,
And time yet for a hundred indecisions,
And for a hundred visions and revisions,
Before the taking of a toast and tea.

In the room the women come and go
Talking of Michelangelo.

And indeed there will be time
To wonder, 'Do I dare?' and, 'Do I dare?'
Time to turn back and descend the stair,
With a bald spot in the middle of my hair –
(They will say: 'How his hair is growing thin!')
My morning coat, my collar mounting firmly to the chin,
My necktie rich and modest, but asserted by a simple pin –
(They will say: 'But how his arms and legs are thin!')
Do I dare
Disturb the universe?
In a minute there is time
For decisions and revisions which a minute will reverse.

For I have known them all already, known them all –
Have known the evenings, mornings, afternoons,
I have measured out my life with coffee spoons;
I know the voices dying with a dying fall
Beneath the music from a farther room.
So how should I presume?

And I have known the eyes already, known them all –
The eyes that fix you in a formulated phrase,
And when I am formulated, sprawling on a pin,
When I am pinned and wriggling on the wall,
Then how should I begin
To spit out all the butt-ends of my days and ways?
And how should I presume?

And I have known the arms already, known them all –
Arms that are braceleted and white and bare
(But in the lamplight, downed with light brown hair!)
Is it perfume from a dress
That makes me so digress?
Arms that lie along a table, or wrap about a shawl.

And should I then presume?
And how should I begin?

.   .   .   .   .

Shall I say, I have gone at dusk through narrow streets
And watched the smoke that rises from the pipes
Of lonely men in shirt-sleeves, leaning out of windows?...

I should have been a pair of ragged claws
Scuttling across the floors of silent seas.

.   .   .   .   .

And the afternoon, the evening, sleeps so peacefully!
Smoothed by long fingers,
Asleep...tired...or it malingers,
Stretched on the floor, here beside you and me.
Should I, after tea and cakes and ices,
Have the strength to force the moment to its crisis?
But though I have wept and fasted, wept and prayed,
Though I have seen my head (grown slightly bald) brought in upon
        a platter,
I am no prophet – and here's no great matter;
I have seen the moment of my greatness flicker,
And I have seen the eternal Footman hold my coat, and snicker,
And in short, I was afraid.

And would it have been worth it, after all,
After the cups, the marmalade, the tea,
Among the porcelain, among some talk of you and me,
Would it have been worth while,
To have bitten off the matter with a smile,
To have squeezed the universe into a ball

To roll it towards some overwhelming question,
To say: 'I am Lazarus, come from the dead,
Come back to tell you all, I shall tell you all' –
If one, settling a pillow by her head,
    Should say: 'That is not what I meant at all.
    That is not it, at all.'

And would it have been worth it, after all,
Would it have been worth while,
After the sunsets and the dooryards and the sprinkled streets,
After the novels, after the teacups, after the skirts that trail along
        the floor –
And this, and so much more? –
It is impossible to say just what I mean!
But as if a magic lantern threw the nerves in patterns on a screen:
Would it have been worth while
If one, settling a pillow or throwing off a shawl,
And turning toward the window, should say:
    'That is not it at all,
    That is not what I meant at all.'

            .   .   .   .   .

No! I am not Prince Hamlet, nor was meant to be;
Am an attendant lord, one that will do
To swell a progress, start a scene or two,
Advise the prince; no doubt, an easy tool,
Deferential, glad to be of use,
Politic, cautious, and meticulous;
Full of high sentence, but a bit obtuse;
At times, indeed, almost ridiculous –
Almost, at times, the Fool.

    I grow old... I grow old...
I shall wear the bottoms of my trousers rolled.

    Shall I part my hair behind? Do I dare to eat a peach?
I shall wear white flannel trousers, and walk upon the beach.
I have heard the mermaids singing, each to each.

I do not think that they will sing to me.

I have seen them riding seaward on the waves
Combing the white hair of the waves blown back
When the wind blows the water white and black.

We have lingered in the chambers of the sea
By sea-girls wreathed with seaweed red and brown
Till human voices wake us, and we drown.

T.S. ELIOT

A Confession

My Lord, I loved strawberry jam
And the dark sweetness of a woman's body.
Also, well-chilled vodka, herring in olive oil,
Scents, of cinnamon, of cloves.
So what kind of prophet am I? Why should the spirit
Have visited such a man? Many others
Were justly called, and trustworthy.
Who would have trusted me? For they saw
How I empty glasses, throw myself on food,
And glance greedily at the waitress's neck.
Flawed and aware of it. Desiring greatness,
Able to recognise greatness wherever it is,
And yet not quite, only in part, clairvoyant,
I know what was left for smaller men like me:
A feast of brief hopes, a rally of the proud.
A tournament of hunchbacks, literature.

CZESŁAW MIŁOSZ
translated by Czeslaw Miłosz & Robert Hass

O Taste and See

The world is
not with us enough.
O taste and see

the subway Bible poster said,
meaning **The Lord**, meaning
if anything all that lives
to the imagination's tongue,

grief, mercy, language.
tangerine, weather, to
breathe them, bite,
savor, chew, swallow, transform

into our flesh our
deaths, crossing the street, plum, quince,
living in the orchard and being

hungry, and plucking
the fruit.

DENISE LEVERTOV

From Blossoms

From blossoms comes
this brown paper bag of peaches
we bought from the boy
at the bend in the road where we turned toward
signs painted *Peaches.*

From laden boughs, from hands,
from sweet fellowship in the bins,
comes nectar at the roadside, succulent
peaches we devour, dusty skin and all,
comes the familiar dust of summer, dust we eat.

O, to take what we love inside,
to carry within us an orchard, to eat
not only the skin, but the shade,
not only the sugar, but the days, to hold
the fruit in our hands, adore it, then bite into
the round jubilance of peach.

There are days we live
as if death were nowhere
in the background; from joy
to joy to joy, from wing to wing,
from blossom to blossom to
impossible blossom, to sweet impossible blossom.

LI-YOUNG LEE

The Simple Truth

I bought a dollar and a half's worth of small red potatoes,
took them home, boiled them in their jackets
and ate them for dinner with a little butter and salt.
Then I walked through the dried fields
on the edge of town. In middle June the light
hung on in the dark furrows at my feet,
and in the mountain oaks overhead the birds
were gathering for the night, the jays and mockers
squawking back and forth, the finches still darting
into the dusty light. The woman who sold me
the potatoes was from Poland; she was someone
out of my childhood in a pink spangled sweater and sunglasses
praising the perfection of all her fruits and vegetables
at the roadside stand and urging me to taste
even the pale, raw sweetcorn trucked all the way,
she swore, from New Jersey. 'Eat, eat,' she said,
'Even if you don't I'll say you did.'
$\qquad\qquad\qquad\qquad\qquad$ Some things
you know all your life. They are so simple and true
they must be said without elegance, meter and rhyme,
they must be laid on the table beside the salt shaker,
the glass of water, the absence of light gathering
in the shadows of picture frames, they must be
naked and alone, they must stand for themselves.
My friend Henri and I arrived at this together in 1965
before I went away, before he began to kill himself,
and the two of us to betray our love. Can you taste
what I'm saying? It is onions or potatoes, a pinch
of simple salt, the wealth of melting butter, it is obvious,
it stays in the back of your throat like a truth
you never uttered because the time was always wrong,
it stays there for the rest of your life, unspoken,
made of that dirt we call earth, the metal we call salt,
in a form we have no words for, and you live on it.

PHILIP LEVINE

Sweetness, Always

Why such harsh machinery?
Why, to write down the stuff
and people of every day,
must poems be dressed up in gold,
in old and fearful stone?

I want verses of felt or feather
which scarcely weigh, mild verses
with the intimacy of beds
where people have loved and dreamed.
I want poems stained
by hands and everydayness.

Verses of pastry which melt
into milk and sugar in the mouth,
air and water to drink,
the bites and kisses of love.
I long for eatable sonnets,
poems of honey and flour.

Vanity keeps prodding us
to lift ourselves skyward
or to make deep and useless
tunnels underground.

So we forget the joyous
love-needs of our bodies.
We forget about pastries.
We are not feeding the world.

In Madras a long time since,
I saw a sugary pyramid,
a tower of confectionery –
one level after another,
and in the construction, rubies,

and other blushing delights,
medieval and yellow.

Someone dirtied his hands
to cook up so much sweetness.

Brother poets from here
and there, from earth and sky,
from Medellín, from Veracruz,
Abyssinia, Antofagasta,
do you know the recipe for honeycombs?

Let's forget all about that stone.

Let your poetry fill up
the equinoctial pastry shop
our mouths long to devour –
all the children's mouths
and the poor adults' also.
Don't go on without seeing,
relishing, understanding
all these hearts of sugar.

Don't be afraid of sweetness.

With us or without us,
sweetness will go on living
and is infinitely alive,
forever being revived,
for it's in a man's mouth,
whether he's eating or singing,
that sweetness has its place.

PABLO NERUDA
translated from the Spanish by Alastair Reid

Happiness

There's just no accounting for happiness,
or the way it turns up like a prodigal
who comes back to the dust at your feet
having squandered a fortune far away.

And how can you not forgive?
You make a feast in honor of what
was lost, and take from its place the finest
garment, which you saved for an occasion
you could not imagine, and you weep night and day
to know that you were not abandoned,
that happiness saved its most extreme form
for you alone.

No, happiness is the uncle you never
knew about, who flies a single-engine plane
onto the grassy landing strip, hitchhikes
into town, and inquires at every door
until he finds you asleep midafternoon
as you so often are during the unmerciful
hours of your despair.

It comes to the monk in his cell.
It comes to the woman sweeping the street
with a birch broom, to the child
whose mother has passed out from drink.
It comes to the lover, to the dog chewing
a sock, to the pusher, to the basket maker,
and to the clerk stacking cans of carrots
in the night.
        It even comes to the boulder
in the perpetual shade of pine barrens,
to rain falling on the open sea,
to the wineglass, weary of holding wine.

JANE KENYON

Trio

Coming up Buchanan Street, quickly, on a sharp winter evening
a young man and two girls, under the Christmas lights –
The young man carries a new guitar in his arms,
the girl on the inside carries a very young baby,
and the girl on the outside carries a chihuahua.
And the three of them are laughing, their breath rises
in a cloud of happiness, and as they pass
the boy says, 'Wait till he sees this but!'
The chihuahua has a tiny Royal Stewart tartan coat like a teapot-
       holder,
the baby in its white shawl is all bright eyes and mouth like favours
       in a fresh sweet cake,
the guitar swells out under its milky plastic cover, tied at the neck
       with silver tinsel tape and a brisk sprig of mistletoe.
Orphean sprig! Melting baby! Warm chihuahua!
The vale of tears is powerless before you.
Whether Christ is born, or is not born, you
put paid to fate, it abdicates
                      under the Christmas lights.
Monsters of the year
go blank, are scattered back,
can't bear this march of three.

– And the three have passed, vanished in the crowd
(yet not vanished, for in their arms they wind
the life of men and beasts, and music,
laughter ringing them round like a guard)
at the end of this winter's day.

EDWIN MORGAN

The Present

For the present there is just one moon,
though every level pond gives back another.

But the bright disc shining in the black lagoon,
perceived by astrophysicist and lover,

is milliseconds old. And even that light's
seven minutes older than its source.

And the stars we think we see on moonless nights
are long extinguished. And, of course,

this very moment, as you read this line,
is literally gone before you know it.

Forget the here-and-now. We have no time
but this device of wantoness and wit.

Make me this present then: your hand in mine,
and we'll live out our lives in it.

MICHAEL DONAGHY

'The washing never gets done...'

The washing never gets done.
The furnace never gets heated.
Books never get read.
Life is never completed.
Life is like a ball which one must continually
catch and hit so that it won't fall.
When the fence is repaired at one end,
it collapses at the other. The roof leaks,
the kitchen door won't close, there are cracks in the foundation,
the torn knees of children's pants...
One can't keep everything in mind. The wonder is
that beside all this one can notice
the spring which is so full of everything
continuing in all directions – into evening clouds,
into the redwing's song and into every
drop of dew on every blade of grass in the meadow,
as far as the eye can see, into the dusk.

JAAN KAPLINSKI
translated from the Estonian by Jaan Kaplinski
with Sam Hamill & Riina Tamm

A Man in His Life

A man doesn't have time in his life
to have time for everything.
He doesn't have seasons enough to have
a season for every purpose. Ecclesiastes
was wrong about that.

A man needs to love and to hate at the same moment,
to laugh and cry with the same eyes,
with the same hands to throw stones and to gather them,
to make love in war and war in love.

And to hate and forgive and remember and forget,
to arrange and confuse, to eat and to digest
what history
takes years and years to do.

A man doesn't have time.
When he loses he seeks, when he finds
he forgets, when he forgets he loves, when he loves
he begins to forget.

And his soul is seasoned, his soul
is very professional.
Only his body remains forever
an amateur. It tries and it misses,
gets muddled, doesn't learn a thing,
drunk and blind in its pleasures
and its pains.

He will die as figs die in autumn,
shrivelled and full of himself and sweet,
the leaves growing dry on the ground,
the bare branches pointing to the place
where there's time for everything.

YEHUDA AMICHAI
translated from the Hebrew by Chana Bloch

Entirely

If we could get the hang of it entirely
    It would take too long;
All we know is the splash of words in passing
    and falling twigs of song,
And when we try to eavesdrop on the great
    Presences it is rarely
That by a stroke of luck we can appropriate
    Even a phrase entirely.

If we could find our happiness entirely
    In somebody else's arms
We should not fear the spears of the spring nor the city's
    Yammering fire alarms
But, as it is, the spears each year go through
    Our flesh and almost hourly
Bell or siren banishes the blue
    Eyes of Love entirely.

And if the world were black or white entirely
    And all the charts were plain
Instead of a mad weir of tigerish waters,
    A prism of delight and pain,
We might be surer where we wished to go
    Or again we might be merely
Bored but in brute reality there is no
    Road that is right entirely.

LOUIS MacNEICE

An Absolutely Ordinary Rainbow

The word goes round Repins,
the murmur goes round Lorenzinis,
at Tattersalls, men look up from sheets of numbers,
the Stock Exchange scribblers forget the chalk in their hands
and men with bread in their pockets leave the Greek Club:
There's a fellow crying in Martin Place. They can't stop him.

The traffic in George Street is banked up for half a mile
and drained of motion. The crowds are edgy with talk
and more crowds come hurrying. Many run in the back streets
which minutes ago were busy main streets, pointing:
There's a fellow weeping down there. No one can stop him.

The man we surround, the man no one approaches
simply weeps, and does not cover it, weeps
not like a child, not like the wind, like a man
and does not declaim it, nor beat his breast, nor even
sob very loudly – yet the dignity of his weeping

holds us back from his space, the hollow he makes about him
in the midday light, in his pentagram of sorrow,
and uniforms back in the crowd who tried to seize him
stare out at him, and feel, with amazement, their minds
longing for tears as children for a rainbow.

Some will say, in the years to come, a halo
or force stood around him. There is no such thing.
Some will say they were shocked and would have stopped him
but they will not have been there. The fiercest manhood,
the toughest reserve, the slickest wit amongst us

trembles with silence, and burns with unexpected
judgements of peace. Some in the concourse scream
who thought themselves happy. Only the smallest children
and such as look out of Paradise come near him
and sit at his feet, with dogs and dusty pigeons.

Ridiculous, says a man near me, and stops
his mouth with his hands, as if it uttered vomit –
and I see a woman, shining, stretch her hand
and shake as she receives the gift of weeping;
as many as follow her also receive it

and many weep for sheer acceptance, and more
refuse to weep for fear of all acceptance,
but the weeping man, like the earth, requires nothing,
the man who weeps ignores us, and cries out
of his writhen face and ordinary body

not words, but grief, not messages, but sorrow,
hard as the earth, sheer, present as the sea –
and when he stops, he simply walks between us
mopping his face with the dignity of one
man who has wept, and now has finished weeping.

Evading believers, he hurries off down Pitt Street.

LES MURRAY

Kindness

Before you know what kindness really is
you must lose things,
feel the future dissolve in a moment
like salt in a weakened broth.
What you held in your hand,
what you counted and carefully saved,
all this must go so you know
how desolate the landscape can be
between the regions of kindness.

How you ride and ride
thinking the bus will never stop,
the passengers eating maize and chicken
will stare out the window forever.

Before you learn the tender gravity of kindness,
you must travel where the Indian in a white poncho
lies dead by the side of the road.
You must see how this could be you,
how he too was someone
who journeyed through the night with plans
and the simple breath that kept him alive.

Before you know kindness as the deepest thing inside,
you must know sorrow as the other deepest thing.
You must wake up with sorrow.
You must speak to it till your voice
catches the thread of all sorrows
and you see the size of the cloth.

Then it is only kindness that makes sense anymore,
only kindness that ties your shoes
and sends you out into the day to mail letters and purchase bread,
only kindness that raises its head
from the crowd of the world to say
It is I you have been looking for,
and then goes with you everywhere
like a shadow or a friend.

NAOMI SHIHAB NYE

One Art

The art of losing isn't hard to master;
so many things seem filled with the intent
to be lost that their loss is no disaster.

Lose something every day. Accept the fluster
of lost door keys, the hour badly spent.
The art of losing isn't hard to master.

Then practice losing farther, losing faster:
places, and names, and where it was you meant
to travel. None of these will bring disaster.

I lost my mother's watch. And look! my last, or
next-to-last, of three loved houses went.
The art of losing isn't hard to master.

I lost two cities, lovely ones. And, vaster,
some realms I owned, two rivers, a continent.
I miss them, but it wasn't a disaster.

– Even losing you (the joking voice, a gesture
I love) I shan't have lied. It's evident
the art of losing's not too hard to master
though it may look like (*Write* it!) like disaster.

ELIZABETH BISHOP

Nothing Is Lost

Nothing is lost. Nothing is so small
that it does not return.
                  Imagine
that as a child on a day like this
you held a newly minted coin and had
the choice of spending it in any way
you wished.
            Today the coin comes back to you,
the date rubbed out, the ancient mottoes vague,
the portrait covered with the dull shellac
of anything used up, passed on, disposed of
with something else in view, and always worth
a little less each time.
              Now it returns,
and you will think it unimportant, lose
it in your pocket change as one more thing
that's not worth counting, not worth singling out.
That is the mistake you must avoid today.
You sent it on a journey to yourself.
Now hold it in your hand. Accept it as
the little you have earned today.
                  And realise
that you must choose again but over less.

DANA GIOIA

The Weighing

The heart's reasons
seen clearly,
even the hardest
will carry
its whip-marks and sadness
and must be forgiven.

As the drought-starved
eland forgives
the drought-starved lion
who finally takes her,
enters willingly then
the life she cannot refuse,
and is lion, is fed,
and does not remember the other.

So few grains of happiness
measured against all the dark
and still the scales balance.

The world asks of us
only the strength we have and we give it.
Then it asks more, and we give it.

JANE HIRSHFIELD

Burlap Sack

A person is full of sorrow
the way a burlap sack is full of stones or sand.
We say, 'Hand me the sack,'
but we get the weight.
Heavier if left out in the rain.
To think that the sand or stones are the self is an error.
To think that grief is the self is an error.
Self carries grief as a pack mule carries the side bags,
being careful between the trees to leave extra room.
The mule is not the load of ropes and nails and axes.
The self is not the miner nor builder nor driver.
What would it be to take the bride
and leave behind the heavy dowry?
To let the thin-ribbed mule browse in tall grasses,
its long ears waggling like the tails of two happy dogs?

JANE HIRSHFIELD

Silence

Silence said:
truth needs no eloquence.
After the death of the horseman,
the homeward-bound horse
says everything
without saying anything.

MOURID BARGHOUTI
translated from the Arabic by Radwa Ashour

A Brief for the Defense

Sorrow everywhere. Slaughter everywhere. If babies
are not starving someplace, they are starving
somewhere else. With flies in their nostrils.
But we enjoy our lives because that's what God wants.
Otherwise the mornings before summer dawn would not
be made so fine. The Bengal tiger would not
be fashioned so miraculously well. The poor women
at the fountain are laughing together between
the suffering they have known and the awfulness
in their future, smiling and laughing while somebody
in the village is very sick. There is laughter
every day in the terrible streets of Calcutta,
and the women laugh in the cages of Bombay.
If we deny our happiness, resist our satisfaction,
we lessen the importance of their deprivation.
We must risk delight. We can do without pleasure,
but not delight. Not enjoyment. We must have
the stubbornness to accept our gladness in the ruthless
furnace of this world. To make injustice the only
measure of our attention is to praise the Devil.
If the locomotive of the Lord runs us down,
we should give thanks that the end had magnitude.
We must admit there will be music despite everything.
We stand at the prow again of a small ship
anchored late at night in the tiny port
looking over to the sleeping island: the waterfront
is three shuttered cafés and one naked light burning.
To hear the faint sound of oars in the silence as a rowboat
comes slowly out and then goes back is truly worth
all the years of sorrow that are to come.

JACK GILBERT

Musée des Beaux Arts

About suffering they were never wrong,
The Old Masters: how well they understood
Its human position; how it takes place
While someone else is eating or opening a window or just walking
        dully along;
How, when the aged are reverently, passionately waiting
For the miraculous birth, there always must be
Children who did not specially want it to happen, skating
On a pond at the edge of the wood:
They never forgot
That even the dreadful martyrdom must run its course
Anyhow in a corner, some untidy spot
Where the dogs go on with their doggy life and the torturer's horse
Scratches its innocent behind on a tree.

In Brueghel's *Icarus*, for instance: how everything turns away
Quite leisurely from the disaster; the ploughman may
Have heard the splash, the forsaken cry,
But for him it was not an important failure; the sun shone
As it had to on the white legs disappearing into the green
Water; and the expensive delicate ship that must have seen
Something amazing, a boy falling out of the sky,
Had somewhere to get to and sailed calmly on.

W.H. AUDEN

The fly

She sat on a willow-trunk
watching
part of the battle of Crécy,
the shouts,

the gasps,
the groans,
the tramping and the tumbling.

During the fourteenth charge
of the French cavalry
she mated
with a brown-eyed male fly
from Vadincourt.

She rubbed her legs together
as she sat on a disembowelled horse
meditating
on the immortality of flies.

With relief she alighted
on the blue tongue
of the Duke of Clervaux.

When silence settled
and only the whisper of decay
softly circled the bodies

and only
a few arms and legs
still twitched jerkily under the trees,

she began to lay her eggs
on the single eye
of Johann Uhr,
the Royal Armourer.

And thus it was
that she was eaten by a swift
fleeing
from the fires of Estrées.

MIROSLAV HOLUB
translated from the Czech by George Theiner

The Place Where We Are Right

From the place where we are right
flowers will never grow
in the spring.

The place where we are right
is hard and trampled
like a yard.

But doubts and loves
dig up the world
like a mole, a plow.
And a whisper will be heard in the place
where the ruined
house once stood.

YEHUDA AMICHAI
translated from the Hebrew by Stephen Mitchell

The Diameter of the Bomb

The diameter of the bomb was thirty centimeters
and the diameter of its effective
range – about seven meters.
And in it four dead and eleven wounded.
And around them in a greater circle
of pain and time are scattered
two hospitals and one cemetery.
But the young woman who was
buried where she came from
over a hundred kilometers away
enlarges the circle greatly.
And the lone man who weeps over her death
in a far corner of a distant country
includes the whole world in the circle.
And I won't speak at all about the crying of orphans
that reaches to the seat of God
and from there onward, making
the circle without end and without God.

YEHUDA AMICHAI
translated from the Hebrew by Yehuda Amichai & Ted Hughes

September Song

born 19.6.32 – deported 24.9.42

Undesirable you may have been, untouchable
you were not. Not forgotten
or passed over at the proper time.

As estimated, you died. Things marched,
sufficient, to that end.
Just so much Zyklon and leather, patented
terror, so many routine cries.

(I have made
an elegy for myself it
is true)

September fattens on vines. Roses
flake from the wall. The smoke
of harmless fires drifts to my eyes.

This is plenty. This is more than enough.

GEOFFREY HILL

All of These People

Who was it who suggested that the opposite of war
Is not so much peace as civilisation? He knew
Our assassinated Catholic greengrocer who died
At Christmas in the arms of our Methodist minister,
And our ice-cream man whose continuing requiem
Is the twenty-one flavours children have by heart.
Our cobbler mends shoes for everybody; our butcher
Blends into his best sausages leeks, garlic, honey;
Our cornershop sells everything from bread to kindling.
Who can bring peace to people who are not civilised?
All of these people, alive or dead, are civilised.

MICHAEL LONGLEY

The Red and the Black

We sat up late, talking –
thinking of the screams of the tortured
and the last silence of starving children,
seeing the faces of bigots and murderers.

Then sleep.

And there was the morning, smiling
in the dance of everything. The collared doves
guzzled the rowan berries and the sea
washed in, so gently, so tenderly.
Our neighbours greeted us
with humour and friendliness.

World, why do you do this to us,
giving us poison with one hand
and the bread of life with another?

And reason sits helpless at its desk,
adding accounts that never balance,
finding no excuse for anything.

NORMAN MacCAIG

Try to Praise the Mutilated World

Try to praise the mutilated world.
Remember June's long days,
and wild strawberries, drops of wine, the dew.
The nettles that methodically overgrow
the abandoned homesteads of exiles.
You must praise the mutilated world.
You watched the stylish yachts and ships;
one of them had a long trip ahead of it,
while salty oblivion awaited others.
You've seen the refugees heading nowhere,
you've heard the executioners sing joyfully.
You should praise the mutilated world.
Remember the moments when we were together
in a white room and the curtain fluttered.
Return in thought to the concert where music flared.
You gathered acorns in the park in autumn
and leaves eddied over the earth's scars.
Praise the mutilated world
and the gray feather a thrush lost,
and the gentle light that strays and vanishes
and returns.

ADAM ZAGAJEWSKI
translated from the Polish by Clare Cavanagh

Sweetness

Just when it has seemed I couldn't bear
   one more friend
waking with a tumor, one more maniac

with a perfect reason, often a sweetness
   has come
and changed nothing in the world

except the way I stumbled through it,
   for a while lost
in the ignorance of loving

someone or something, the world shrunk
   to mouth-size,
hand-size, and never seeming small.

I acknowledge there is no sweetness
   that doesn't leave a stain,
no sweetness that's ever sufficiently sweet...

Tonight a friend called to say his lover
   was killed in a car
he was driving. His voice was low

and guttural, he repeated what he needed
   to repeat, and I repeated
the one or two words we have for such grief

until we were speaking only in tones.
   Often a sweetness comes
as if on loan, stays just long enough

to make sense of what it means to be alive,
   then returns to its dark
source. As for me, I don't care

where it's been, or what bitter road
    it's traveled
to come so far, to taste so good.

STEPHEN DUNN

Though There Are Torturers

Though there are torturers in the world
There are also musicians.

Though, at this moment,
Men are screaming in prisons
There are jazzmen raising storms
Of sensuous celebration
And orchestras releasing
Glories of the Spirit.

Though the image of God
Is everywhere defiled
A man in West Clare
Is playing the concertina,
The Sistine Choir is levitating
Under the dome of St Peter's
And a drunk man on the road
Is singing for no reason.

MICHAEL COADY

It's This Way

I stand in the advancing light,
my hands hungry, the world beautiful.

My eyes can't get enough of the trees –
they're so hopeful, so green.

A sunny road runs through the mulberries,
I'm at the window of the prison infirmary.

I can't smell the medicines –
carnations must be blooming nearby.

It's this way:
being captured is beside the point,
the point is not to surrender.

NÂZIM HIKMET
translated from the Turkish by Randy Blasing & Mutlu Konuk

Hijab Scene #7

No, I'm not bald under the scarf
No, I'm not from that country
where women can't drive cars
No, I would not like to defect
I'm already American
But thank you for offering
What else do you need to know
relevant to my buying insurance,
opening a bank account,
reserving a seat on a flight?
Yes, I speak English
Yes, I carry explosives
They're called words
And if you don't get up
Off your assumptions,
They're going to blow you away

MOHJA KAHF

They'll say, 'She must be from another country'

When I can't comprehend
why they're burning books
or slashing paintings,
when they can't bear to look
at god's own nakedness,
when they ban the film
and gut the seats to stop the play
and I ask why
they just smile and say,
'She must be
from another country.'

When I speak on the phone
and the vowel sounds are off
when the consonants are hard
and they should be soft,
they'll catch on at once
they'll pin it down
they'll explain it right away
to their own satisfaction,
they'll cluck their tongues
and say,
'She must be
from another country.'

When my mouth goes up
instead of down,
when I wear a tablecloth
to go to town,
when they suspect I'm black
or hear I'm gay
they won't be surprised,
they'll purse their lips
and say,
'She must be
from another country.'

When I eat up the olives
and spit out the pits
when I yawn at the opera
in the tragic bits
when I pee in the vineyard
as if it were Bombay,
flaunting my bare ass
covering my face
laughing through my hands
they'll turn away,
shake their heads quite sadly,
'She doesn't know any better,'
they'll say,

'She must be
from another country.'

Maybe there is a country
where all of us live,
all of us freaks
who aren't able to give
our loyalty to fat old fools,
the crooks and thugs
who wear the uniform
that gives them the right
to wave a flag,
puff out their chests,
put their feet on our necks,
and break their own rules.

But from where we are
it doesn't look like a country,
it's more like the cracks
that grow between borders
behind their backs.
That's where I live.
And I'll be happy to say,
'I never learned your customs.
I don't remember your language
or know your ways.
I must be
from another country.'

IMTIAZ DHARKER

Aubade

I work all day, and get half-drunk at night.
Waking at four to soundless dark, I stare.
In time the curtain-edges will grow light.
Till then I see what's really always there:
Unresting death, a whole day nearer now,
Making all thought impossible but how
And where and when I shall myself die.
Arid interrogation: yet the dread
Of dying, and being dead,
Flashes afresh to hold and horrify.

The mind blanks at the glare. Not in remorse
– The good not done, the love not given, time
Torn off unused – nor wretchedly because
An only life can take so long to climb
Clear of its wrong beginnings, and may never;
But at the total emptiness for ever,
The sure extinction that we travel to
And shall be lost in always. Not to be here,
Not to be anywhere,
And soon; nothing more terrible, nothing more true.

This is a special way of being afraid
No trick dispels. Religion used to try,
That vast moth-eaten musical brocade
Created to pretend we never die,
And specious stuff that says *No rational being
Can fear a thing it will not feel*, not seeing
That this is what we fear – no sight, no sound,
No touch or taste or smell, nothing to think with,
Nothing to love or link with,
The anaesthetic from which none come round.

And so it stays just on the edge of vision,
A small unfocused blur, a standing chill
That slows each impulse down to indecision.
Most things may never happen: this one will,
And realisation of it rages out
In furnace-fear when we are caught without
People or drink. Courage is no good:
It means not scaring others. Being brave
Lets no one off the grave.
Death is no different whined at than withstood.

Slowly light strengthens, and the room takes shape.
It stands plain as a wardrobe, what we know,
Have always known, know that we can't escape,
Yet can't accept. One side will have to go.
Meanwhile telephones crouch, getting ready to ring
In locked-up offices, and all the uncaring
Intricate rented world begins to rouse.
The sky is white as clay, with no sun.
Work has to be done.
Postmen like doctors go from house to house.

PHILIP LARKIN

Common and Particular

I like these men and women who have to do with death,
Formal, gentle people whose job it is,
They mind their looks, they use words carefully.

I liked that woman in the sunny room
One after the other receiving such as me
Every working day. She asks the things she must

And thanks me for the answers. Then I don't mind
Entering your particulars in little boxes,
I like the feeling she has seen it all before,

There is a form, there is a way. But also
That no one come to speak up for a shade
Is like the last, I see she knows that too.

I'm glad there is a form to put your details in,
Your dates, the cause. Glad as I am of men
Who'll make a trestle of their strong embrace

And in a slot between two other slots
Do what they have to every working day:
Carry another weight for someone else.

It is common. You are particular.

DAVID CONSTANTINE

114

Funeral Blues

Stop all the clocks, cut off the telephone,
Prevent the dog from barking with a juicy bone,
Silence the pianos and with muffled drum
Bring out the coffin, let the mourners come.

Let aeroplanes circle moaning overhead
Scribbling on the sky the message He Is Dead,
Put crêpe bows round the white necks of the public doves,
Let the traffic policemen wear black cotton gloves.

He was my North, my South, my East and West,
My working week and my Sunday rest,
My noon, my midnight, my talk, my song;
I thought that love would last for ever: I was wrong.

The stars are not wanted now: put out every one;
Pack up the moon and dismantle the sun;
Pour away the ocean and sweep up the wood.
For nothing now can ever come to any good.

W.H. AUDEN

Memorial

Everywhere she dies. Everywhere I go she dies.
No sunrise, no city square, no lurking beautiful mountain
but has her death in it.
The silence of her dying sounds through
the carousel of language, it's a web
on which laughter stitches itself. How can my hand
clasp another's when between them
is that thick death, that intolerable distance?

She grieves for my grief. Dying, she tells me
that bird dives from the sun, that fish
leaps into it. No crocus is carved more gently
than the way her dying
shapes my mind. But I hear, too,
the other words,
black words that make the sound
of soundlessness, that name the nowhere
she is continuously going into.

Ever since she died
she can't stop dying. She makes me
her elegy. I am a walking masterpiece,
a true fiction
of the ugliness of death.
I am her sad music.

NORMAN MacCAIG

Darling

You might forget the exact sound of her voice
or how her face looked when sleeping.
You might forget the sound of her quiet weeping
curled into the shape of a half moon,

when smaller than her self, she seemed already to be leaving
before she left, when the blossom was on the trees
and the sun was out, and all seemed good in the world.
I held her hand and sang a song from when I was a girl –

Heel y'ho boys, let her go boys –
and when I stopped singing she had slipped away,
already a slip of a girl again, skipping off,
her heart light, her face almost smiling.

And what I didn't know or couldn't say then
was that she hadn't really gone.
The dead don't go till you do, loved ones.
The dead are still here holding our hands.

JACKIE KAY

Eden Rock

They are waiting for me somewhere beyond Eden Rock:
My father, twenty-five, in the same suit
Of Genuine Irish Tweed, his terrier Jack
Still two years old and trembling at his feet.

My mother, twenty-three, in a sprigged dress
Drawn at the waist, ribbon in her straw hat,
Has spread the stiff white cloth over the grass.
Her hair, the colour of wheat, takes on the light.

She pours tea from a Thermos, the milk straight
From an old H.P. sauce bottle, a screw
Of paper for a cork; slowly sets out
The same three plates, the tin cups painted blue.

The sky whitens as if lit by three suns.
My mother shades her eyes and looks my way
Over the drifted stream. My father spins
A stone along the water. Leisurely,

They beckon to me from the other bank.
I hear them call, 'See where the stream-path is!
Crossing is not as hard as you might think.'

I had not thought that it would be like this.

CHARLES CAUSLEY

Gravy

No other word will do. For that's what it was. Gravy.
Gravy, these past ten years.
Alive, sober, working, loving and
being loved by a good woman. Eleven years
ago he was told he had six months to live
at the rate he was going. And he was going
nowhere but down. So he changed his ways
somehow. He quit drinking! And the rest?
After that it was *all* gravy, every minute
of it, up to and including when he was told about,
well, some things that were breaking down and
building up inside his head. 'Don't weep for me,'
he said to his friends. 'I'm a lucky man.
I've had ten years longer than I or anyone
expected. Pure gravy. And don't forget it.'

RAYMOND CARVER

Prayer

May things stay the way they are
in the simplest place you know.

May the shuttered windows
keep the air as cool as bottled jasmine.
May you never forget to listen
to the crumpled whisper of sheets
that mould themselves to your sleeping form.
May the pillows always be silvered
with cat-down and the muted percussion
of a lover's breath.
May the murmur of the wall clock
continue to decree that your providence
run ten minutes slow.

May nothing be disturbed
in the simplest place you know
for it is here in the foetal hush
that blueprints dissolve
and poems begin,
and faith spreads like the hum of crickets,
faith in a time
when maps shall fade,
nostalgia cease
and the vigil end.

ARUNDATHI SUBRAMANIAM

from Four Quartets

FROM East Coker

I [extract]

In my beginning is my end. In succession
Houses rise and fall, crumble, are extended,
Are removed, destroyed, restored, or in their place
Is an open field, or a factory, or a by-pass.
Old stone to new building, old timber to new fires,
Old fires to ashes, and ashes to the earth
Which is already flesh, fur and faeces,
Bone of man and beast, cornstalk and leaf.
Houses live and die: there is a time for building
And a time for living and for generation
And a time for the wind to break the loosened pane
And to shake the wainscot where the field-mouse trots
And to shake the tattered arras woven with a silent motto.

In my beginning is my end. Now the light falls
Across the open field, leaving the deep lane
Shuttered with branches, dark in the afternoon,
Where you lean against a bank while a van passes,
And the deep lane insists on the direction
Into the village, in the electric heat
Hypnotised. In a warm haze the sultry light
Is absorbed, not refracted, by grey stone.
The dahlias sleep in the empty silence.
Wait for the early owl.

V [extract]

Home is where one starts from. As we grow older
The world becomes stranger, the pattern more complicated
Of dead and living. Not the intense moment
Isolated, with no before and after,
But a lifetime burning in every moment
And not the lifetime of one man only

But of old stones that cannot be deciphered.
There is a time for the evening under starlight,
A time for the evening under lamplight
(The evening with the photograph album).
Love is most nearly itself
When here and now cease to matter.
Old men ought to be explorers
Here or there does not matter
We must be still and still moving
Into another intensity
For a further union, a deeper communion
Through the dark cold and the empty desolation,
The wave cry, the wind cry, the vast waters
Of the petrel and the porpoise. In my end is my beginning.

FROM Little Gidding

V

What we call the beginning is often the end
And to make an end is to make a beginning.
The end is where we start from. And every phrase
And sentence that is right (where every word is at home,
Taking its place to support the others,
The word neither diffident nor ostentatious,
An easy commerce of the old and the new,
The common word exact without vulgarity,
The formal word precise but not pedantic,
The complete consort dancing together)
Every phrase and every sentence is an end and a beginning,
Every poem an epitaph. And any action
Is a step to the block, to the fire, down the sea's throat
Or to an illegible stone: and that is where we start.
We die with the dying:
See, they depart, and we go with them.
We are born with the dead:
See, they return, and bring us with them.

The moment of the rose and the moment of the yew tree
Are of equal duration. A people without history
Is not redeemed from time, for history is a pattern
Of timeless moments. So, while the light fails
On a winter's afternoon, in a secluded chapel
History is now and England.

With the drawing of this Love and the voice of this Calling

We shall not cease from exploration
And the end of all our exploring
Will be to arrive where we started
And know the place for the first time.
Through the unknown, unremembered gate
When the last of earth left to discover
Is that which was the beginning;
At the source of the longest river
The voice of the hidden waterfall
And the children in the apple tree
Not known, because not looked for
But heard, half-heard, in the stillness
Between two waves of the sea.
Quick now, here, now, always –
A condition of complete simplicity
(Costing not less than everything)
And all shall be well and
All manner of thing shall be well
When the tongues of flame are in-folded
Into the crowned knot of fire
And the fire and the rose are one.

T.S. ELIOT

Postscript

And some time make the time to drive out west
Into County Clare, along the Flaggy Shore,
In September or October, when the wind
And the light are working off each other
So that the ocean on one side is wild
With foam and glitter, and inland among stones
The surface of a slate-grey lake is lit
By the earthed lightning of a flock of swans,
Their feathers roughed and ruffling, white on white,
Their fully grown headstrong-looking heads
Tucked or cresting or busy underwater.
Useless to think you'll park and capture it
More thoroughly. You are neither here nor there,
A hurry through which known and strange things pass
As big soft buffetings come at the car sideways
And catch the heart off guard and blow it open.

SEAMUS HEANEY

Late Fragment

And did you get what
you wanted from this life, even so?
I did.
And what did you want?
To call myself beloved, to feel myself
beloved on the earth.

RAYMOND CARVER

APPENDICES

NOTES ON POETS AND POEMS

While poetry should speak for itself, some background can be helpful to new readers or when encountering particular poets or poems for the first time. In compiling these notes, I've tried to balance those two aspects, saying little where little is needed but offering a sketch, a gloss or a short commentary where this feels appropriate.

Kim Addonizio (*b*. Washington, DC, 1954) is an American poet of Italian and tennis-playing descent whose passions and readings include blues harmonica. Her other interests: 'Sex and death are right up there. Consciousness, which I guess is really the subject of all writing. Life on earth, in a body that's going to decay and die, while everything changes and changes again. Being caught in time. The world beyond the world, or within it.' [*Slow Trains* interview.] ➡ 'For Desire' [60], 'You Don't Know What Love Is' [61].

Agha Shahid Ali (1949-2001) was born in Srinagar and educated in Kashmir and Delhi. After moving to the United States, he described himself as 'Kashmiri-American' not Indian-American, as Jeet Thayil has noted: 'He would on occasion let the pose slip: "I never apologise, shameless little Indian that I am." For Americans, he was an impossibly exotic figure: a self-professed product of three cultures, Muslim, Hindu and Western, and a permanent "triple exile". In contrast to the flamboyance of his personality, his subject was grief – for a vanished landscape or the death of a loved one – and his last book of poems *Rooms Are Never Finished* (2001) was in large part an elegy to his mother, Sufia, who died of brain cancer. He would die of the same illness ("I will die that day in late October, it will be long ago").' [*The Bloodaxe Book of Contemporary Indian Poets.*] ➡ 'Stationery' [73].

Yehuda Amichai (1924-2000) was Israel's greatest modern poet, and one of the first to write in colloquial Hebrew. Born in Würzberg, Germany, he emigrated with his family at the age of 11. Widely translated, his poetry is both public and personal, ironic and playfully serious, secular but God-engaged, concerned with love and life as well as war and political engagement: 'Dealing with political realities is part of what we need to do to survive as normal human beings.[...] I've often said that all poetry is political. This is because real poems deal with a human response to reality and politics is part of reality, history in the making. Even if a poet writes about sitting in a glass house drinking tea it reflects politics.' [*Paris Review* interview.] ➡ 'A Man in His Life' [88], The Place Where We Are Right' [100], 'The Diameter of the Bomb' [101].

W.H. Auden (*b*. York, 1907-73) was the foremost English poet of the 20th century, influencing a whole generation of politically engaged writers in the 1930s. His poetry's central themes are love, politics, religion, morals, the individual human being and the impersonality of nature. His poem 'Funeral Blues' [➡ 115] gained wide popularity after its recital at a funeral in the film *Four Weddings and a Funeral.* ➡ 'Musée des Beaux Arts' [98].

The Palestinian poet **Mourid Barghouti** (*b*. Deir Ghassana, 1944) has spent much of his life in exile, in Jordan, Lebanon and Egypt. He said this of his poem 'Silence' [➡ 96]: 'When I started the opening two lines of this very short poem, I realised I was talking to myself, not to my readers, as if to solidify my hatred of rhetoric and eloquence and my love for simplicity and concrete language. As a Palestinian with a negated history and a threatened geography, craving world attention and understanding, I was hesitant to have the poem published. But I decided to publish it because I needed to be its reader. I was trying to convince Mourid Barghouti that pain, even the Palestinian pain, does not mean shouting loudly.' [*Guardian*, 13 December 2008.]

Coleman Barks (*b*. Chattanooga, Tennessee, 1937) is an American poet renowned as a translator of Rumi [➡ 13, 151] and other mystic poets. He has been a student of Sufism since 1977. Working from literal, scholarly transcriptions of Persian poetry (and with John Moyne in particular), he produces what he calls 'collaborative translations': 'I try to create valid English free verse in American English... I try to be aware of what spiritual information is trying to come through.' Barks has managed 'to connect these poems with a strong American line of free-verse spiritual poetry', such as that of Theodore Roethke, Gary Snyder, Walt Whitman and James Wright.

Elizabeth Bishop (1911-79) is now recognised as one of the greatest poets of the 20th century. When she died in 1979, she had only published four collections, yet had won virtually every major American literary award. She maintained close friendships with poets such as Marianne Moore and Robert Lowell, and was always highly regarded by other writers, but her work has only come to eclipse that of her contemporaries in the years since her death.

Born in Worcester, Massachusetts, she was a virtual orphan from an early age, brought up by relatives in New England and Nova Scotia. The tragic circumstances of her life – from alcoholism to repeated experiences of loss in her relationships with women – nourished an outsider's poetry notable both for its reticence and tentativeness. Her closely observed poetry mirrors the ambivalence she perceived in the world, 'the always-more-successful surrealism of everyday life', transforming the world through close observation as though seeing is believing.

Her insights are achieved through acute observation. 'At the Fishhouses' [➡ 38] shows poetry's transforming power, Bishop's accumulation of minute detail leading to the incantatory finale where the sea is described as like knowledge, 'flowing and drawn, and since / our knowledge is historical, flowing, and flown'. That word 'flown' is the past participle not of 'flow' but of 'fly'; 'flown', chiming with 'drawn', sounds better than 'flowed', but completely changes the sense. James Merrill, Anne Stevenson, Robert Pinsky and George Szirtes have all written illuminating commentaries on these few lines.

Robert Frost wrote that 'Poetry provides the one permissible way of saying one thing and meaning another'. A prime example of that would be Bishop's villanelle 'One Art' [➡ 93], which claims 'The art of losing isn't hard to master', but the effect of its repeatedly rhymed assertions is to assert the opposite, with the parenthesised interjection ('*Write* it!') brilliantly disrupting the clinching last line. Indirection and understatement can often provide a stronger means of expressing and confronting a conflict between thought and feeling than open lament or direct description.

John Burnside (*b*. Dunfirmline, Fife, 1955) is a Scottish writer of radiant, meditative poetry and of dark, brooding fiction. His books include several collections of poetry and one of short stories, several novels, and a memoir, *A Lie About My Father* (2006). In his essay in *Strong Words* (2000), he wrote: 'Our response to the world is essentially one of wonder, confronting the mysterious with a sense, not of being small, or insignificant, but of being part of a rich and complex narrative.' ➡ 'Unwittingly' [44]; *from* 'Of Gravity and light' [72].

Edip Cansever (*b*. Istanbul, 1928-86) went from school into business at his father's antiques shop in Istanbul, later lamenting he hadn't studied philosophy: 'At nineteen I was married, and at twenty I was a young man with a child. I was at the same time obliged to make a living, and drawn to poetry. [...] My partner was a good-hearted man. He was in charge of sales, while I would read and write in the mezzanine. Our true friendship began in those days with poetry and continued for twenty-two years. The results are in my home, my room and among my books.' ['Autobiographical Sketch', *Irish Pages*, 4 no.1.] Cansever became one of Turkey's leading post-war poets.

First published in 1954 in his second book of poems, 'Table' [➡15] became a talismanic poem for Turkish readers but was a mixed blessing for its author: he said if he had written nothing other than this poem, 'it would have been worth it. And yet I haven't been able to escape from this poem ever in my life.'

Translators Julia and Richard Tillinghast: 'Cansever's imagination is a place where physical objects, sense impressions and ideas coexist not only with ease, but with joy.[...] But if Cansever is not religious, he is, in a strikingly unacademic way, a philosophical poet. Who other than a philosophical poet could have written these lines in "Precipice": "O appearances, there's something about you I just don't understand!" In "Table" we suspect he was thinking of Plato's "forms", and that his table represents something like the Platonic idea of a table.[...] The poem is given some background by the knowledge that Cansever owned an antique shop in the Covered Bazaar, so he must have bought and sold many an old table that wobbled but then stood firm.' ['Neither Hopeless Nor Not Hopeless: At Cansever's Table', *Irish Pages*, 4 no.1.]

Raymond Carver (*b*. Clatskanie, Oregon, 1938-88) viewed Chekhov as common soul in his practice both as a poet and a highly influential short story writer. His stories chronicle the lives of marginalised people in smalltown America, while his poems tell stories about difficult marriages, strained relationships and dealing with illness. Winning his own personal battle with alcoholism, he found happiness late in life with the poet Tess Gallagher – the gift of ten more years he celebrates in 'Gravy' [➡ 119] – only to be defeated by lung cancer. The poem 'Late Fragment' [➡ 124] is inscribed on his grave.

Nina Cassian (*b*. Galati, Romania, 1924) is a Romanian poet, journalist and classical composer. She was granted asylum in the US when a friend was arrested by the Securitate in 1985 for possessing a diary including poems by her satirising the Ceausescu régime. Her poetry is highly personal and courageous, with passion as its central concern: passion as desire and passion as suffering. She believes that poetry 'is not to transcend life or to transform it, but it is life...Art is as alive as an animal.' ➡ 'Temptation' [25].

Charles Causley (1917-2003) lived for most of his life in his birthplace, Launceston in Cornwall, where he worked as a schoolteacher, and produced many books for children and six poetry collections. He said he couldn't tell when writing if a poem was for children or for adult readers, and included children's poetry in his 1975 *Collected Poems*. His poetry is both traditional and visionary, drawing on timeless forms such as ballads, folksongs and hymns. ➡ 'Eden Rock' [118].

C.P. Cavafy (*b*. Alexandria, Egypt, 1863-1933) was a Greek poet who lived in Egypt, where he worked as a journalist and civil servant. His poetry was little known outside the Greek community of Alexandria, only winning critical recognition in Greece itself after his death and wider international renown much later with the publication of numerous translations into other languages. Cavafy divided his poems into three categories: philosophical, historical and hedonistic or aesthetic, the eroticism of the latter emerging as explicitly homosexual only after 1918. Common to all his mature work is his 'unique tone of voice' which, according to Auden, 'survives translation'. 'Ithaka' [➡ 28] is his quintessential life-quest poem in which the journey itself is what's important, not the final landing (the Laistrygonians and the Cyclops were giants encountered by Odysseus on his ten-year odyssey after the Trojan War).

Julius Chingono (*b*. Norton, Zimbabwe, 1946-2011), the son of a farmworker, worked for most of his life as a blaster on the mines. Made redundant in 1999, he worked intermittently as a rock-blasting contractor. His poem 'As I Go' [➡ 27] depicts a life stripped to its essentials. 'His often deceptively simple poetry was written with compassion and clarity, feeling deeply as he did for the hardships of the poor and marginalised, while his honesty, humour and ironic eye made him a sharp and witty observer of those who abused their station through corruption and hypocrisy.' [*Poetry International Web*]

Kate Clanchy (*b*. Glasgow, 1965) is a poet whose work has had a mixed reception, earning immediate recognition with her first book, *Slattern* (1995), but unjustified, damaging attacks by male critics for her otherwise much admired and popular third collection, *Newborn* (2004), which 'draws on common experiences of women, and the unfamiliar world they enter once they have boarded the pregnancy train and realise, to use Sylvia Plath's metaphor, that "there's no getting off" [Deryn Rees-Jones]. ➡ 'Love' [50].

Michael Coady (*b*. Carrick-on-Suir, Co. Tipperary, Ireland, 1939) is a poet, short story writer and photographer whose work explores the universal in the local, celebrating town and country, people and place in Ireland. ➡ 'Though There Are Torturers' [107].

David Constantine (*b.* Salford, 1944) is an English poet known also for his translations of poets such as Enzensberger, Goethe, Hölderlin and Jaccottet. Like the work of the European poets who have nourished him, his poetry is informed by a profoundly humane vision of the world. Throughout his work, the personal life, with its own joys and suffering, asserts itself against a world whose characteristic forces are dispiriting and destructive. For Constantine, all personal life and all poetry written from it deal with the realities of social and political life in the here and now, assert themselves, fight for survival, and actively seek to make a world in which humane self-realisation would be more and more, not less and less, possible. 'Common and Particular' [➡ 114].

Imtiaz Dharker is a poet, artist and documentary filmmaker. Her cultural experience spans three countries: born in Lahore, Pakistan, in 1954, she grew up a Muslim Calvinist in Glasgow, later eloping with a Hindu Indian to live in Bombay. She now lives between India and Britain, drawing her main themes from a life of transitions: childhood, exile, journeying, home, religious strife and terror. Her poetry has universal appeal, especially in these times. When I read her poem 'They'll say, "She must be from another country"' [➡ 109] at the launch reading for the American edition of *Staying Alive* at New York's Cooper Union in 2003, the whole audience of several hundred people burst into spontaneous applause.

Michael Donaghy (*b.* New York City, 1954-2004) was an Irish-American poet and musician who moved to London in his 30s, and was a phenomenal reader of his work. His playfully serious poetry owed much to the example of 17th-century Metaphysical poets like John Donne, often elaborating an unusual metaphor or combination of metaphors through many narrative shifts and surprises, much to the delight of audiences at his *tour-de-force* performances. His sudden death at the age of 50 came as a great shock to his many friends in the poetry community in Britain. ➡ 'The Present' [86].

Mark Doty (*b.* Maryville, Tennessee, 1953) is an American writer noted for the compassion, relish and wild muscularity of his highly personal poetry. Central to Doty's work are animals and his concern for the need to cope nobly and gracefully with what is beyond our control. Exploring our preoccupation with the past and the future, he encourages us to live more in the present. His poetry universalises themes of loss, mortality and renewal, and expresses a remarkable empathy for all human and animal life. He has published several collections, including *My Alexandria* (1993) and *Atlantis* (1995), which deal poignantly with the failing health and ultimate death of his partner from AIDS and with his almost crippling grief – also the subject of his prose memoir *Heaven's Coast* (1996). ➡ 'Migratory' [34].

Rita Dove (*b*. Akron, Ohio, 1952), the daughter of one of the first black chemists to work in America's tyre industry, was the youngest US Poet Laureate (in 1993-95) and to date the only African-American poet to hold that office. Her poetry is known for its lyricism as well as for its personalised sense of history, political scope and diverse themes, from the Civil Rights era to music and dance. She edited the eclectic *Penguin Anthology of 20th Century American Poetry* (2011). ➡ 'Dawn Revisited' [18].

Alan Dugan (*b*. New York City, 1923-2003) was an idiosyncratic American poet who titled all his collections *Poems*, culminating in *Poems Seven* in 2001. His poetry is ironic and down-to-earth, his language skilfully drawing on everyday speech, his stance often disenchanted, at odds with society and despairing of the world, but accepting what is necessary for survival, especially in love and marriage, as in 'Love Song: I and Thou' [➡ 63]

Helen Dunmore is an English poet, novelist and children's writer who won the first Orange Prize for fiction in 1996. Born in Beverley, Yorkshire, in 1952, she has lived in Bristol for most of her life, but the place which has exerted the greatest pull on her imagination has been Cornwall: the land, the sea and the light. Her poems capture the fleetingness of life, its sweetness and intensity, the short time we have on earth and the pleasures of the earth, with death as the frame which sharpens everything and gives it shape. ➡ 'Wild strawberries' [58].

Stephen Dunn (*b.* New York City, 1939) started out as a semi-professional basketball player, worked in advertising and served in the US Army, experiences which must have helped ground his poetry, with its concern with the anxieties, joys and problems of how to co-exist in the world with those who are part of our daily lives. No fewer than five poems in *Staying Alive*, including 'Sweetness' [➤ 106], were taken from his 1989 collection, *Between Angels*, a book remarkable for its portrayal of 'our human vulnerability and our quiet everyday tenacity, perhaps courage, in the face of those vulnerabilities' [Steve Kronen, *Kenyon Review*].

T.S. Eliot (*b.* St Louis, Missouri, 1888-1965) was the foremost Modernist poet of the 20th century, raised in America but writing his greatest work after moving to England. His two major works are *The Waste Land* (1922) and *Four Quartets* (1943), the former written when he was 'classical in literature, royalist in politics, and Anglo-Catholic in religion' (as he wrote in 1928), the latter after his conversion to Anglicanism.

Like *The Waste Land*, 'The Love Song of J. Alfred Prufrock' [➤ 74] is a densely allusive work, presenting 'a psychological landscape where inner obsessions mesh with outer conditions' [Edna Longley]. Eliot's poetry includes quotations from many classic poems, often in the original language, expressing the universality of particular human experiences. His epigraph to 'Prufrock' is from the *Inferno* (XXVII, 61-66), where Dante recounts his visit to the underworld. These words are spoken by Count Guido da Montefelltro (1223-98), punished in a prison of flame for his treachery on earth: 'If I thought that my reply would be to someone who would ever return to earth, this flame would remain without further movement; but as no one has ever returned alive from this gulf, if what I hear is true, I can answer you with no fear of infamy.'

George Orwell preferred Eliot's earlier poetry of 'glowing despair' to the later 'melancholy faith' of his wartime sequence *Four Quartets*, which mystically blends an Anglican version of Englishness with the 'way' to God. The extracts here are from two of the *Quartets*, 'East Coker' [➤ 121] and 'Little Gidding [➤ 122], named after English villages he visited during the 1930s, one with family associations and the other an Anglican community.

U.A. Fanthorpe (*b*. Kent, 1929-2009) began writing while working as a hospital receptionist, publishing her first collection, *Side Effects* (1978), at the age of 49. She was Head of English at Cheltenham Ladies' College when she made a life-changing decision to become 'a middle-aged drop-out in order to write': 'At once I'd found the subject that I'd been looking for all my life: the strangeness of other people, particularly neurological patients, and how it felt to be them, and to use their words.' Looking back later, she realised that behind all her poems 'lie preoccupations with the way people speak, birds, the landscape, cats, England, power, powerlessness and words, words, words'. ➡ 'Atlas' [62].

Robert Frost (*b*. San Francisco, 1874-1963) was the most popular American poet of the 20th century. Most of his best-known poems are set in the New Hampshire farmland where he lived. Joseph Brodsky said of Frost (1996): 'He is generally regarded as the poet of the countryside, of rural settings – as a folksy, crusty, wisecracking old gentleman farmer, generally of positive disposition. In short, as American as apple pie.[…] Now, this is obviously a romantic caricature.[…] Nature, for this poet, is neither friend nor foe, nor is it the backdrop for human drama; it is this poet's terrifying self-portrait.'

When Nehru lay dying, he had written out the last verse of Robert Frost's 'Stopping by Woods on a Snowy Evening' [➡ 33] on a piece of paper by his bed, and kept repeating the lines ('And miles to go before I sleep…'). Another Frost poem, 'The Road Not Taken' [➡ 31], became America's favourite modern poem because it encapsulates everyone's anxieties about the roads we take – or might have taken – in life. Many of the *Staying Alive* trilogy poems dramatise these kinds of life decisions: the journeys we take, the roads we choose or have chosen for us.

Little-known outside America, **Jack Gilbert** (*b*. Pittsburgh, 1925) is a latterday metaphysical poet whose work replays the myth of Orpheus and Eurydice, recurrent figures in his books. Gilbert's poetry bears witness to what he calls 'the craft of the invisible', that is, form in the service of his explosive content. James Dickey calls him 'a necessary poet': 'He takes himself away to a place more inward than it is safe to go; from that awful silence and tightening, he returns to us poems of savage compassion.' ➤ 'A Brief for the Defense' [97].

Dana Gioia (*b.* Los Angeles, 1950) is an American writer of Italian and Mexican descent. He retired early from a career as a corporate executive at General Foods to write full-time, was a revitalising chairman of the National Endowment for the Arts for six years, and is now Professor of Poetry and Public Culture at the University of Southern California. A leading New Formalist poet, he is also a critic and outspoken literary commentator, with books including the controversial *Can Poetry Matter?* (1992). His highly musical poetry is quietly visionary, often showing human lives rooted in the natural world. ➤ 'Nothing Is Lost' [94].

Lars Gustafsson is a prolific Swedish poet, novelist, scholar and outspoken social critic, best-known for his novel *Death of a Beekeeper* (1978). Born in Västerås in 1936, he taught philosophy and literature at the University of Texas at Austin for over 25 years, and now divides his time between Stockholm, Bullaren and Berlin. His poetry registers the metaphysical alongside the mundane with a particular kind of clarity that has come to be associated with his work. Illuminating the potency of ordinary objects and everyday events, Gustafsson addresses critical issues that have concerned great thinkers over the centuries. Asked where he finds his inspiration, Gustafsson replied: 'I listen. I listen and I look. Creativity knows no rules. You can get an idea for a novel from a little something someone says, or just a face you see. A rabbi once told me that when God spoke to Moses in that bush, it wasn't in a thundering voice; it was in a very weak voice. You have to listen carefully for that voice. You have to be very sharp.' [*Nordic Reach,* XX no.21, 2008] ➤ 'The Girl' [45].

Kerry Hardie (*b.* Singapore, 1951) is an Irish writer who has published six books of poetry and two novels. Often following the annual round of rural life, her poetry questions, celebrates and challenges all aspects of life and experience, exploring the mystery of 'why we are here', but is ultimately concerned with the quiet realisation that 'there is nothing to do in the world except live in it'. A number of her poems are narratives or parables in which experience yields a spiritual lesson and consolation; others chart a coming to terms with death or continuing illness and an acceptance of inevitability or flux. Human life quivers in consort with other lives in these seasons of the heart. 'In many of these poems, illness opens into a compassionate understanding of suffering and death, familial and historical [...] she finds in nature a redemptive power for the body, prompting the big questions of human and divine purpose.' [Selina Guinness, *The New Irish Poets*]. ➡ 'Sheep Fair Day' [70].

Seamus Heaney (*b*. Mossbawn, Co. Derry, 1939) is a world-renowned Irish poet and critic, the winner of the Nobel Prize in Literature in 1995. Born into a Catholic farming family in Co. Derry, he left Northern Ireland in 1972 and has since lived in America, Wicklow and Dublin. His concerns for the land, language and troubled history of Ireland run through all of his work. His early poetry is notable for its sensory, lyrical evocations of nature and rural life, and of childhood, which has nurtured many of his most memorable poems, as Heaney has acknowledged: 'My poems almost always start in some kind of memory [...] like a little beeper going off in your mind. Some little thing wakens excitement, and it gets connected with some other things. Ideally, it's like an avalanche – a little pebble begins to move, gathers a lot of energy and multiplies itself.' ➡ *from* 'Clearances' [48], 'Postscript' [24].

Turkey's most celebrated modern poet, **Nâzim Hikmet** (1902-63), served thirteen years of a 28-year-sentence as a political prisoner, accused of inciting Turkish armed forces to revolt because military cadets had been reading his poems. He was only freed after a worldwide campaign, with protests led by Picasso, Paul Robeson and Jean-Paul Sartre adding international pressure to turmoil created by his hunger strikes. Hikmet's poem 'It's This Way' [➡ 108] was written in 1948 from the prison infirmary. Still persecuted after his release, he spent his last thirteen years in exile in Russia. His work was banned in Turkey for thirty years and has been translated into more than fifty languages.

Born in Thessaloniki (then Selânik, part of the Ottoman Empire), Hikmet grew up in Istanbul. After fighting in the Turkish War of Independence, he spent part of the early 1920s in Moscow, witnessing revolutionary politics and influenced by Mayakovsky and the new Soviet poets. On his return to Turkey, he became the foremost figure in the Turkish avant-garde, known for his innovative poetry's unusual synthesis of iconoclasm and lyricism, ideology and poetic diction.

'In prison, Hikmet's Futurist-inspired, often topical early poetry gave away to poems with a more direct manner and a more serious tone.[...] He not only composed some of his greatest lyrics in prison but produced, between 1941 and 1945, his epic masterwork, *Human Landscapes*,' wrote Mutlu Konuk. According to Terrence Des Pres, Hikmet's 'exemplary life' and 'special vision' – 'at once historical and timeless, Marxist *and* mystical' meant that 'in his art and in his person Hikmet opposes the enemies of the human spirit in harmony with itself and the earth'. Reading Hikmet, said Carolyn Forché, we are in the presence of 'a rare guide to the work of remaining hopeful and in love with life, pure of heart and human, passionate and dedicated to the common good'. [*Poems of Nâzim Hikmet*, tr. Randy Blasing & Mutlu Konuk, 1994/2002]

Sir Geoffrey Hill is widely regarded as Britain's greatest living poet. Born in Bromsgrove, Worcestershire, in 1932, he read English at Oxford. He taught at Leeds University from 1954 to 1980, and thereafter at Cambridge and Boston. He was made Oxford Professor of Poetry in 2010, and was knighted in 2012.

Hill's densely allusive poetry has earned him a reputation for "difficulty" which he has defended as the poet's right in the face of cultural disintegration, political opportunism and media-driven mediocrity, arguing that to be difficult is to be democratic and equating the demand for simplicity with the demands of tyrants. His approach to "difficulty" includes subjecting his own lyricism to intense interrogation and self-questioning, as in 'September Song' [➡ 102], an early poem written for an unknown child who died anonymously in one or other concentration camp. Throughout this oblique and understated poem, Hill writes with an acute awareness of how the Nazis perfected the art of misusing language to disguise the nature of their 'Final Solution', simultaneously masking and revealing the horror behind that phrase through painful irony, awful double-meanings and juxtapositions ('routine cries'), so that the meaning of each line changes, or shifts, with each line-break.

Jane Hirshfield is a visionary American poet who trained as a Zen Buddhist. Born in New York City in 1953, she has lived in northern California since 1974, for the past 20 years in a small white cottage looking out on fruit trees, old roses and Mt Tamalpais. Her poems are both sensual meditations and passionate investigations which reveal complex truths in language luminous and precise. Rooted in the living world, they celebrate and elucidate a hard-won affirmation of our human fate. ➤ 'The Weighing' [95], 'Burlap Sack' [96].

Miroslav Holub (*b*. Pilsen, Czechoslovakia, 1923-98) was the Czech Republic's foremost modern poet, and one of her leading immunologists. Often employing scientific metaphors, his fantastical and witty poems give a scientist's bemused view of human folly and other life on the planet. ➤ 'The door' [19], 'The fly' [98].

Langston Hughes (*b*. Joplin, Missouri, 1902-67) was a key figure in the Harlem Renaissance of the 1920s. A poet, novelist, short story writer and dramatist, he was known for his vivid portrayals of black life in America as well as for his engagement with the world of jazz. Resisting demands from younger and militant black writers to be a political spokesman, Hughes maintained a belief in humanity and tolerance which ensured that his poetry remained universal in its appeal while staying relevant to the plight of his downtrodden people. ➤ 'Harlem [2]' [21].

Mohja Kahf (*b*. Damascus, 1967) is an Arab-American writer who moved with her family from Syria to the US when she was a child. Her interest in morality, gender, politics and how Muslim-American communities relate to others in both religious and secular spheres finds expression in her poetry, fiction and academic studies. Her collection *Emails from Scheherazad* (2003) draws on the Arabic oral tradition and Arabic poetry as well as

American free verse, and includes 'Hijab Scene #7' [➡ 109], one of a series of poems on that theme.

Jaan Kaplinski (*b*. Tartu, Estonia, 1941) is one of Europe's major poets, and one of his country's best-known writers and cultural figures. His philosophical poetry shows the influence of European Modernism, classical Chinese poetry and Buddhist philosophy. Also a linguist, translator, sociologist and ecologist, he lectured on the history of Western civilisation at Tartu University and was a member of the Estonian parliament in 1992-95. His essays on cultural transition and the challenges of globalisation are published across the Baltic region. ➡ 'The washing never gets done...' [87].

Doris Kareva is one of Estonia's leading poets. Born in Tallinn in 1958, she studied Roman-Germanic philology at Tartu University. She has published many collections of poetry, her work has been translated into over 20 languages, and she is herself a distinguished translator who has translated the work of writers such as Akhmatova, Emily Dickinson, Gibran, Kabir, Auden, Brodsky, Beckett and Shakespeare into Estonian. Her *Shape of Time* [➡ 12] is a book-length sequence composed like a piece of music in three movements. In her introduction to its English edition (2010), Penelope Shuttle writes: 'Doris Kareva observes the anguish of existence and experience in a style that is pared-back, bone-clean, needle-sharp. Her work has indeed the notation of the music of inwardness, of its despairs and its mediating flashes of illumination. And thus her poetry has its being in a time and place where past, present and future exist simultaneously.'

Jackie Kay (*b*. Edinburgh, 1961) was an adopted child of Scottish/Nigerian parentage brought up by a white Communist couple in Glasgow, the background of her first book of poems, *The Adoption Papers* (1991). Her poetry draws on her own life and the lives of others to make a tapestry of voice and communal understanding. She has published several books of poetry, two collections of short stories, a novel, a memoir, plays and books for children. ➡ 'Darling' [117].

Brendan Kennelly is an Irish poet, critic and dramatist who taught at Trinity College Dublin for over 30 years. Born in 1936, he grew up in the village of Ballylongford in Co. Kerry, and most of his work is concerned with the people, landscapes, wildlife and history of Ireland, and with language, religion and politics. Best-known for three controversial poetry books, *Cromwell* (1983), *The Book of Judas* (1991) and *Poetry My Arse* (1995), he is a much loved public figure in Ireland, and a popular guest on television programmes. His poem 'Begin' [➡ 26] was widely circulated by Irish Americans in the aftermath of 9/11, and Meryl Streep chose to read it at the launch reading for the American edition of *Staying Alive* in New York in 2003. 'His poems shine with the wisdom of somebody who has thought deeply about the paradoxical strangeness and familiarity and wonder of life' [Sister Stanislaus Kennedy].

Jane Kenyon (*b*. Ann Arbor, Michigan, 1947-95) was an American poet who fought depression and other illnesses for much of her life. Her quietly musical poems are compassionate meditations intently probing the life of the heart and spirit. Observing and absorbing small miracles in everyday life, they grapple with fundamental questions of human existence. ➡ 'Otherwise' [20], 'Happiness' [84].

Galway Kinnell (*b*. Providence, Rhode Island, 1927) is an American poet whose diverse work ranges from odes of kinship with nature to realistic evocations of urban life, from religious quest to political statement, from brief imagistic lyrics to extended, complex meditations. Many of his poems examine the effects of personal confrontation with violence and inevitable death, attempts to hold death at bay, the plight of the urban dispossessed, and the regenerative powers of love and nature. He is 'America's pre-eminent visionary', and his poetry 'greets each new age with rapture and abundance [and] sets him at the table with his mentors: Rilke, Whitman, Frost' [National Book Award citation, 2003]. ➡ 'After Making Love We Hear Footsteps' [54].

Stanley Kunitz (*b*. Worcester, Massachusetts, 1905-2006) was a highly influential American poet, editor, translator and teacher committed to fostering community amongst artists. His poetry is autobiographical but also fiercely visionary. Drawing on Jungian symbolism, he engaged with personal tragedy and public conscience to produce a resilient poetry of testing wisdom. His last work, published on his 100th birthday, was *The Wild Braid: A Poet Reflects on a Century in the Garden* (2005), a gathering of poems and photographs from the garden he created over 40 years at his summer home in Provincetown, Cape Cod, interwoven with Kunitz's reflections on poetry, nature, life, death and the creative process. ➡ 'The Layers' [29].

Philip Larkin (*b*. Coventry, 1922-85) was an influential and popular English poet, the leading figure in the 'Movement' group whose plain-speaking, descriptive poetry using traditional forms was the dominant poetic mode in British poetry of the 1950s and early 60s. His main themes are love, marriage, freedom, destiny, loss, ageing and death. Influenced by Yeats, Eliot, Auden and Hardy, Larkin was a late Romantic lyric poet who evolved a persona suited to his pessimistic postwar outlook on life: dry, sceptical, modest and unshowy, thinking aloud in an apparently commensensical fashion, yet also honest, emotional and capable of rich surprises of thought and imagery. Also a novelist and jazz critic, he worked in Hull in the university library for the last 30 years of his life.

Seamus Heaney calls Larkin's 'Aubade' [➡ 112] 'the definitive post-Christian English poem, one that abolishes the soul's traditional pretension to immortality', yet an absence of life after death is as questionable as its presence. Larkin's poem copes with the eternal subject of death, says Czesław Miłosz, 'in a manner corresponding to the second half of the twentieth century', and yet it 'leaves me not only dissatisfied but indignant [...] poetry by its very essence has always been on the side of life. Faith in life everlasting has accompanied man in his wanderings through time and has always been larger and deeper than religious or philosophical creeds.' Heaney says that in imagining death, poetry brings human existence into a fuller life. [*The Redress of Poetry* (1995).] ➡ 'An Arundel Tomb' [64], 'Aubade' [112].

Li-Young Lee was born in 1957 in Jakarta, Indonesia, of Chinese parents. His great-grandfather, Yuan Shikai, was China's first republican president (1912-16). His father, Lee Kuo Yuan, a deeply religious Christian physician, was personal secretary to Communist leader Mao Tse-tung. After they fell out, Lee's father escaped to Indonesia, where he helped found Gamaliel University, but was later imprisoned for 19 months in Sukarno's jails and in a leper colony, before he managed to escape and take his family out of the country. After a five-year trek through Hong Kong, Macau and Japan, they settled in the United States in 1964, where Lee's father became a Presbyterian minister. Assisting his father on preaching trips in Pennsylvania was another of Li-Young Lee's formative experiences. That turbulent background is transformed in his redemptive poetry, which fuses memory, family, culture and history to explore love, exile, family and mortality, searching for understanding and for the right language to give form to what is invisible and evanescent. ➡ 'From Blossoms' [80].

Denise Levertov (*b*. Ilford, Essex, 1923-97), one of the 20th century's foremost American poets, was born in England, the daughter of a Russian Jewish scholar turned Anglican priest and a Welsh Congregationalist mother, both parents descended from mystics. She emigrated to the US in 1948, where she became involved with the Objectivist and Black Mountain schools of poetry, and was much influenced by the work of William Carlos Williams, a lifelong friend and correspondent. Her poetry is notable for its visionary approach to the natural world and to the dynamics of being human. 'Meditative and evocative, Levertov's poetry concerns itself with the search for meaning. She sees the poet's role as a priestly one; the poet is the mediator between ordinary people and the divine mysteries' [Susan J. Zeuenbergen].

Many of poems in the *Staying Alive* trilogy celebrate the joy of living, the beauty of the natural world and the pleasures of the body and the senses. Denise Levertov's 'Living' [➡ 14] captures the vitality of nature and the preciousness of every life and every minute of life, while 'O Taste and See' [➡ 79] tells how the world 'is not with us enough', urging us to connect with 'all that lives' through all our senses.

Philip Levine (*b*. Detroit, 1928) is an American poet of Russian-Jewish immigrant stock viewed by many as the authentic voice of America's urban poor. Born and raised in Detroit, he spent his early years doing a succession of heavy labouring jobs. He taught for over 30 years at California State University, Fresno, and was US Poet Laureate in 2011-12. Much of his poetry addresses the joys and sufferings of industrial life, with radiant feeling as well as painful irony. Always a poet of memory and invention, Levine has continually written poems which search for universal truths. His plain-speaking poetry is a testament to the durability of love, the strength of the human spirit and the persistence of life in the face of death. His books include 17 collections of poetry, two books of essays and his recent UK selection, *Stranger to Nothing: Selected Poems* (2006). ➛ 'Starlight' [47], 'The Simple Truth' [81].

Michael Longley (*b*. Belfast, 1939) is an Irish poet of English parentage who has spent most of his life in Belfast and at his second home at Carrigskeewan on the coast of Co. Mayo. A dedicated naturalist, he studied Classics at Trinity College Dublin, and worked for the Arts Council of Northern Ireland from 1970 to 1991. Longley's poetry is formally inventive and precisely observed, spanning and blending love poetry, war poetry, nature poetry, elegies, satires, verse epistles, art and the art of poetry. He has extended the capacity of the lyric to absorb dark matter: the Great War, the Holocaust, the Northern Irish 'Troubles'; and his translations from classical poets speak to contemporary issues. ➛ 'All of These People' [103].

Thomas Lux (*b*. Northampton, Massachusetts, 1946) grew up on his family's dairy farm, later becoming an acclaimed university teacher and writer. After starting out as a Neo-surrealist poet in the 1970s, he 'drifted away from Surrealism and the arbitrariness of that. I got more interested in subjects, identifiable subjects other than my own angst or ennui or things like that. I paid more and more attention to the craft. Making poems rhythmical and musical and believable as human speech and as distilled and tight as possible is very important to me.' [*Cortland Review* interview, 1999] That distillation is clearly evident in 'A

Little Tooth' [➡ 53], which pans through a whole life in nine tightly rhymed lines.

Norman MacCaig (*b.* Edinburgh, 1910-96) always lived in Edinburgh but had family links with the island of Scalpay and often visited Assynt in Sutherland, the setting of his Highlands poems. He worked as a schoolteacher for 30 years, and was a central figure in Edinburgh's often fractious postwar literary set. Mac-Caig studied Classics at Edinburgh University, a strong formal influence behind the precision and lucidity of the poetry he wrote after shaking off the 'Apocalyptic' style of 1940s poetry. The surprising metaphorical conceits which were the hallmark of much of his mature poetry predated the less inventive contrivances of the English 'Martian poets' of the 1980s by decades. ➡ 'The Red and the Black' [104], 'Memorial' [116].

Louis MacNeice (1907-63) was born in Belfast, the son of a rector (later a bishop), and educated in England. He worked as a BBC writer-producer for 20 years, and died from pneumonia after going down pot-holes to record sound effects for a radio play. Somewhat overshadowed by his friend W.H. Auden during the 1930s, MacNeice is the quintessential poet of flux, openness and possibilities. Many of his poems defend individual freedom and tolerance, and kick against conformism and restrictive ideologies. In 'Snow' [➡ 41], he writes that: 'World is crazier and more of it than we think, / Incorrigibly plural. I peel and portion / A tangerine and spit the pips and feel / The drunkenness of things being various.' In 'Entirely' [➡ 89], written over half a century ago when the threat was from fascism or communism, MacNeice opposes the fundamentalist view of the world as 'black or white entirely', seeing life as 'a mad weir of tigerish waters / A prism of delight and pain', which is very much the world view expressed by many different writers throughout the *Staying Alive* trilogy, not just in poems on global or social issues but in highly personal love poems, meditations and elegies.

Derek Mahon (*b.* Belfast, 1941) is the most formally accomplished Irish poet of a generation including Seamus Heaney and Michael Longley. His early influences included Yeats, MacNeice and Beckett along with the French poets he has continued to translate. Mahon's 'A Disused Shed in Co. Wexford' [➡ 42] is one of the great poems of the 20th century. It doesn't just make you pause for thought as you read and re-read it, it almost makes you feel more human. The poem's evolving interplay between thought and feeling – enacted through its engagement with language – produces a delicately balanced response in the reader. Those particular sensations of sound and symbol evoked by this poem trouble the meaning, but you shouldn't expect to understand any poem at one reading. Just as you listen to songs – or sing them – again and again, so poems need to be read, re-read, read out loud and read again. Of all the poems in this anthology, the ones which I feel give the most with each re-reading are those by Derek Mahon, Elizabeth Bishop, Geoffrey Hill and T.S. Eliot.

The mushrooms in Mahon's 'Disused Shed' have been waiting in the dark 'since civil war days'. Their presence is symbolic, standing for all the marginalised people and mute victims of history. Charged with meaning and remembrance by the poem, this forgotten shed behind the rhododendrons is an imagined lost world ('one of those places where a thought might grow') remembered from *Troubles* (1970), a novel set just after the First World War in the decaying Majestic Hotel in rural Ireland by J.G. Farrell, to whom the poem is dedicated (Mahon's friend was a polio victim, and died in Ireland in a drowning accident not long after the poem was written). Written during the Irish 'Troubles' in the 1970s, the poem is both timeless and timely, as Seamus Deane points out: 'It is a poem that heartbreakingly dwells on and gives voice to all those peoples and civilisations that have been lost and/or destroyed. Since it is set in Ireland, with all the characteristics of an Irish "Big House" ruin, it speaks with a special sharpness to the present moment and the fear, rampant in Northern Ireland, of communities that fear they too might perish and be lost, with none to speak for them.'

Mahon's poem achieves its remarkable effects through sound, beginning with a mellifluous evocation through consonance and assonance of fading sounds in the first stanza, through which the first sentence unspools to the metre like a rollcall, with a breath-jump across the stanza gap at the end of line 10, not meeting the first full-stop until the end of the 13th line of the poem, at the light-giving keyhole. Edna Longley's close reading of this poem shows how from this point 'rhythms expressive of the mushrooms crowding to the poem's keyhole, of growth and accumulation, answer those of diminuendo', and also how complementary rhythms trace the 'posture' of 'expectancy' and 'desire' asserted in the narrative. The ten-line stanzas which Mahon handles with such delicacy and consummate skill are "big houses" of his own building indebted to past models, to his formal masters W.B. Yeats and Louis MacNeice.

Czesław Miłosz (*b*. Lithuania, 1911-2004) was Poland's foremost modern poet, often described as a poet of memory and witness. Born in Lithuania (then ruled by Tsarist Russia), he worked for underground presses in Nazi-occupied Warsaw, later becoming a diplomat and given political asylum in France in 1951. He received the Nobel Prize in Literature in 1980. ➡ 'Encounter' [38], 'A Confession' [78].

Edwin Morgan (*b*. Glasgow, 1920-2010) was not only one of the foremost Scottish poets of the 20th century but also one of the most versatile English-language poets and translators of any period, an intellectual polymath with a relish for both traditional forms and for concrete or sound poetry. The vitality and breadth of his work owes much to his voracious appetite for life and literature, his immersion in Russian, French and many other languages, his engagement with art, film, science and science fiction, and his belief that 'you can write poetry about anything. You really can! The world, history, society, everything in it, pleads to become a voice, voices'. ➡ 'Strawberries' [59], 'Trio' [85].

Les Murray (*b*. Nabiac, NSW, 1938) is Australia's best-known poet, a prolific and popular but controversial writer. Encompassing all Australian life – including the natural world – his poetry is dramatic and highly engaging, enlivened by humour and self-mockery, plain-speaking but also complex. While wedded to traditional verse, he is an inventive and exuberant poet: invigorating the ballad form, 'translating' voices from nature into poetry, imitating Aboriginal songs. Like America's Walt Whitman he champions his own 'vernacular republic', but his critics accuse him of blinkered nationalism and reactionary rural conservatism.

Murray's poem 'An Absolutely Ordinary Rainbow' [➡ 90] is about not being afraid to show our emotions: giving physical expression to the way we feel, here by crying in public. There's also a sense of mystery in this: no one knows why the man is crying, and Murray evokes the baffled, communal response to a spectacle both ordinary and extraordinary by echoing a famous poem by 'Waltzing Matilda' author 'Banjo' Paterson in his opening lines. Every Australian of Murray's generation would know by heart 'The Man from Snowy River' which begins: 'There was movement at the station, for the word had passed around / That the colt from old Regret had got away', but instead of bushmen from different cattle-stations, Murray homes in on men reacting from familiar Sydney locations, drinking or eating in Repins and Lorenzinis, or watching the horse sales at Tattersalls.

Pablo Neruda (*b*. Parral, Chile, 1904-73), known in Chile as 'the people's poet', was one of the greatest and most influential poets of the 20th century, and received the Nobel Prize in Literature in 1971. He served his country as a diplomat for many years, but also spent long periods in exile. His poetry embraces both private and public concerns: he is known both for his love and nature poetry and for works addressing Latin American political history and social struggle. His early poetry was fiercely surreal, reflecting ancient terrors, modern anxieties and his near-religious desolation. The Spanish Civil War changed his life and work as he moved to a personal voice and to more politically involved and ideological positions.

The turning-point came with his epic volume *Canto general* (1950), including 'The Heights of Macchu Picchu', which marked 'a new stage in my style and a new direction in my concerns'. Standing on the hallowed Inca ground, Neruda vowed to make the stones speak on behalf of those who had built and laboured on it. What had begun as a poem about Chile turned into one that expressed the whole geological, natural and political history of South America.

His later work was elemental in its concerns, including the three books of *Odes*, which gave material things a life of their own. Nothing was ordinary in Neruda's poetry: anything could be magical; womanhood was linked to the regeneration of earth and the cyclical processes of nature. ➡ 'Sweetness, Always' [82].

Alden Nowlan (*b*. Nova Scotia, 1933-83) is Canada's most popular modern poet, widely celebrated for his heart-warming, plain-speaking poems. Born in the Nova Scotia backwoods, he left school at 12 and worked in a sawmill before becoming a local newspaper reporter. His early poems bear witness to the harshness and hypocrisy of lives brutalised by poverty and ignorance in a remote Canadian backwater. But as Nowlan finds love and lifelong friendship, so his work achieves authority and lasting warmth. His poems present universal portrayals of human life: teasingly ironic, wryly humorous, sympathetic, quizzical and morally astute. 'Great Things Have Happened' [➡ 55].

Naomi Shihab Nye (*b*. St Louis, Missouri, 1952) is an American writer, anthologist, educator and 'wandering poet'. Born to a Palestinian father and an American mother, she has published over 20 books. She gives voice to her experience as an Arab-American through poems about heritage and peace that overflow with a humanitarian spirit. Through her empathetic use of poetic language, she reveals the shining nature of our daily lives, whether writing about local life in her inner-city Texan neighbourhood or the daily rituals of Jews and Palestinians in the war-torn Middle East. ➡ 'Kindness' [91].

Dennis O'Driscoll (*b*. Co. Tipperary, 1954) is an Irish poet, critic and anthologist who has worked as a civil servant since the age of 16. He is a poet of humanity whose wittily observant poetry is attuned to the tragedies and comedies of contemporary life. ➡ 'Missing God' [67].

Sharon Olds (*b*. San Francisco, 1942) is an American poet noted for the candour and brutal honesty of her unflinching poems about love, sex, women and difficult family relationships, but she distinguishes her 'apparently personal poetry' from that of the Confessional poets: 'I have an old-fashioned vision of the word confession. I believe that a confession is a telling, publicly or privately, of a wrong that one has done, which one regrets. And the confession is a way of trying to get to the other side and change one's nature. So I have written two or three confessional poems. I would use the phrase apparently personal poetry for the kind of poetry that I think people are referring to as "confessional". Apparently personal because how do we really know? We don't.' [*Poets & Writers Magazine*, 1993] ➡ 'This Hour' [56].

Mary Oliver (*b*. Ohio, 1935) is America's most popular contemporary poet. Her luminous poetry celebrates nature and beauty, love and the spirit, silence and wonder, extending the visionary American tradition of Whitman, Emerson and Emily Dickinson. It is nourished by her intimate knowledge and minute daily observation of the New England coast around Cape Cod, its woods and ponds, its birds, animals, plants and trees. ➡ 'Wild Geese' [11], 'The Journey' [22].

Alice Oswald (*b*. England, 1966) is probably the most distinctively individual English poet of her generation. Trained as a classicist, she later worked as a gardener, and now lives in Devon. Her poetry is highly musical, often concerned with the natural world, drawing on the English oral tradition and oral history as well as on Homer and Greek mythology. Since *Dart* (2002), each of her books has differed greatly from its predecessor, being conceived as a coherent work of imagination, complete in itself and a powerful testament to the importance of its subject. ➡ 'Wedding' [64].

Fernando Pessoa (*b*. Lisbon, 1888-1935) lived in Lisbon for most of his life, and died in obscurity there, but is now recognised as one of the most innovative and radical literary figures in modern poetry. He wrote under numerous "heteronyms", literary alter egos with their own identities and writing styles, who supported and criticised each other in the literary journals. The poem here [➡ 14] was published by Pessoa as an ode by Ricardo Reis.

Rainer Maria Rilke (*b*. Prague, 1875-1926) was one of the greatest poets of the 20th century. His poetry addresses questions of how to live and relate to the world in a voice that is simultaneously prophetic and intensely personal. Most of his major work was written in German, including the *Duino Elegies* and *Sonnets to Orpheus*. Born in Prague, he lived in France from 1902 and then Switzerland from 1919 until his death. ➡ 'Archaic Torso of Apollo' [22].

Jelaluddin **Rumi** (*b*. Wakhsh, Persia, 1207-73) was a Sufi mystic and poet, born in what is now Tajikistan, who founded the ecstatic dancing order known as the Mevlevi or Whirling Dervishes. Rumi would recite his poems in any place, sometimes day and night for several days, with his disciple Husam writing them down. ➡ 'The Guest House' [13]. *See also* Coleman Barks.

Gjertrud Schnackenberg (*b*. Tacoma, Washington, 1953) is a American poet known for the sensuous richness of her imaginatively daring poetry of ideas and 'her stunning command of prosody' (Eliza Griswold). She has published four collections featuring extended sequences relating to history, art, literature, myth, philosophy and human suffering, and two book-length sequences, *The Throne of Labdacus* (2000), and *Heavenly Questions* (2010/2011), a setting of six long poems of passion, mourning and redemption. ➡ 'Snow Melting' [57].

Ken Smith (*b*. Rudston, Yorkshire, 1938-2002) was an English poet whose work and example inspired a whole generation of younger poets. His poetry shifted territory with time, from rural Yorkshire, America and London to the war-ravaged Balkans and Eastern Europe (before and after Communism). His early books span a transition from a preoccupation with land and myth to his later engagement with urban Britain and the politics of radical disaffection. Smith grew up in the North Riding of Yorkshire, the son of an itinerant farm labourer, and his poem 'Being the third song of Urias' [➡ 46] is written from both these perspectives, evoking the boy back in the raw landscape of his childhood as well as the grown-up man looking back at his life, examining his feelings of separation from the inarticulate, unloving father he sought to understand in this and other poems.

William Stafford (*b*. Kansas, 1914-93) was an American poet who published his first collection at the age of 48. His contemplative poetry celebrates human virtues and universal mysteries, with nature, war, technology and Native American people as his abiding themes. In a typical Stafford poem he seeks an almost sacred place in the wilderness untouched by man, finding meaning in the quest itself and its implications. ➡ 'The Way It Is' [32].

Anne Stevenson (*b*. Cambridge, England, 1933) is an American and British poet, born in Cambridge of American parents, who grew up in the States but has lived in Britain for most of her adult life. Rooted in close observation of the world and acute psychological insight, her poems continually question how we see and think about the world. They are incisive as well as entertaining, marrying critical rigour with personal feeling, and a sharp wit with an original brand of serious humour. ➡ 'Poem for a Daughter' [49], 'The Victory' [51].

Ruth Stone (*b*. Roanoke, Virginia, 1915-2011) lived in rural Vermont for much of her life. After her husband's suicide in 1959, she had to raise three daughters alone, all the time writing what she called her 'love poems, all written to a dead man' who forced her to 'reside in limbo' with her daughters. She only won wide recognition for her work in her late 80s, and was still writing poetry of extraordinary variety and radiance well into her 90s – fierce feminist and political poems and hilarious send-ups, meditations on ageing, love and loss.

Ruth Stone once said, 'I decided very early on not to write like other people.' Her late retrospective *What Love Comes To* (2008/2009) shows the fruits of this resolve in the lifetime's work of a true American original, whose writing process was unlike anyone else's: 'I wrote my first poem without knowing I'd done it – and found that poems came with this mysterious feeling, a kind of peculiar ecstasy. I'd feel and hear a poem coming from a long way off, like a thunderous train of air. I'd feel it physically. I'd run like hell to the house, blindly groping for pencil and paper. And then the poem would write itself. I'd write it down from the inside out. The thing knew itself already. There were other times when I'd almost miss it, feeling it pass through me just as I was grabbing the pencil, but then I'd catch it by its tail and pull it backwards into my body. Then the poem came out backwards and I'd have to turn it round.' [*PBS Bulletin*, 2009] ➤ 'Second-Hand Coat' [16].

Arundhathi Subramaniam (*b.* Bombay, 1967) is an Indian writer whose poems explore various ambivalences – around human intimacy with its bottlenecks and surprises, life in a Third World megalopolis, myth, the politics of culture and gender, and the persistent trope of the existential journey. ➤ 'Prayer' [120].

Anna T. Szabó is one of Hungary's leading younger poets. Born in 1972 in Kolozsvár/Cluj-Napoca in Transylvania (Romania), she moved with her family to Hungary in 1987, later studying English and Hungarian literature at the University of Budapest and obtaining her PhD in English Renaissance literature. She published her first book of poems at the age of 23, and has since published several others as well as translations of writers such as James Joyce, Sylvia Plath, W.B. Yeats and John Updike. She is one of the key figures in George Szirtes' anthology *New Order: Hungarian Poets of the Post 1989 Generation* (2010); her selection there includes 'She Leaves Me' [➤ 52].

Wisława Szymborska (*b.* Bnin, Poland, 1923-2012) was one of Poland's four great 20th-century poets. She won the Nobel Prize in Literature in 1996 'for poetry that with ironic precision allows the historical and biological context to come to light in fragments of human reality'. Her mostly short poems are concerned with large existential issues, exploring the human condition with sceptical wit and ironic understatement. ➤ 'Could Have' [17].

Toon Tellegen was born in Brielle in the Netherlands in 1941. He is a leading Dutch poet as well as a novelist and children's author, and worked as a GP until his recent retirement. His tragicomic poems convey human predicaments with great economy and vitality, often rendering them in the form of dramatic stories or dreamlike events, as in 'I drew a line…' [➤ 32].

R.S. Thomas (1913-2000) was one of the major poets of our time as well as one of the finest religious poets in the English language and Wales's greatest poet. Born in Cardiff, he was an Anglican priest, an isolated figure who worked in only three rural parishes over a lifetime. Most of his poetry covers ground he treads repeatedly: man and God, science and nature, time and history, the land and people of Wales. ➤ 'The Bright Field' [73].

The winner of the Nobel Prize in Literature in 2011, Sweden's **Tomas Tranströmer** (*b*. Stockholm, 1931) is Scandinavia's best-known and most influential contemporary poet, and worked as a psychologist for 30 years. His poems are often explorations of the borderland between sleep and waking, between the conscious and unconscious states. Many use compressed description and concentrate on a single distinct image as a catalyst for psychological insight and metaphysical interpretation. This acts as a meeting-point or threshold between conflicting elements or forces: sea and land, man and nature, freedom and control, as in the poem included here, 'Alone' [➤ 36].

His translator Robin Fulton has noted how such images 'leap out from the page, so that the first-time reader or listener has the feeling of being given something very tangible, at once', which has made Tranströmer's poetry amenable to translation into other languages. Fulton's authoritative English translations of his work are published in Tranströmer's *New Collected Poems* (1997/2011) in Britain, the American edition of which is titled *The Great Enigma* (2006).

Derek Walcott (*b*. St Lucia, 1930) is not only the foremost Caribbean poet writing today (as well as a dramatist and painter) but a major figure in world literature, recognised with the award of the Nobel Prize in Literature in 1992 'for a poetic *œuvre* of great luminosity, sustained by a historical vision, the outcome of a multicultural commitment'. Most of his work explores the Caribbean cultural experience, the history, landscape and lives of its multiracial people, fusing folk culture and oral tales with the classical, avant-garde and English literary tradition. ➤ 'Love after Love' [66].

James Wright (*b*. St Martin's Ferry, Ohio, 1927-80) was one of the most influential American poets of the 20th century. Whether drawing on his native Ohio, the natural world, or the luminous resonant Italy of his later work, his powerful yet vulnerable voice embraces many facets of human experience through shifting tones and moods, both lyric and ironic, autobiographical and social. ► 'Lying in a Hammock at William Duffy's Farm in Pine Island, Minnesota' [24].

Adam Zagajewski was born in 1945 in Lwów (or Lvov), a largely Polish city that became part of the Soviet Ukraine shortly after his birth. His ethnic Polish family, who had lived for centuries in Lwów, were then forcibly repatriated to Poland. He came to prominence as a leading figure in Poland's Generation of '68 or *Nowa Fala* (New Wave), and was later active in the Solidarity movement. After living in France from 1982 and also teaching in the US, he now divides his time between Kraków and Chicago. His luminous, searching poems are imbued by a deep engagement with history, art, and life.

The New Yorker published Zagajewski's 'Try to Praise the Mutilated World' [► 105] on its back page shortly after 11 September 2001. It was a recent poem, not written in response to the Al-Qaeda attacks but was viewed as such, being given such prominent publication at just that time, and certainly took on new resonance in the aftermath to 9/11. In an interview in *Poets & Writers*, Zagajewski said: 'Don't we use the word poetry in two ways? One: as a part of literature. Two: as a tiny part of the world, both human and pre-human, the part of beauty. So poetry as literature, as language, discovers within the world a layer that has existed unobserved in reality, and by doing so changes something in our life, expands somewhat the space of what we are. So yes, it has the power to restore the mutilated world, even if no statistics ever show it.'

ACKNOWLEDGEMENTS

The poems in this anthology are reprinted from the following books, all by permission of the publishers listed unless stated otherwise. Thanks are due to all the copyright holders cited below for their kind permission:

Kim Addonizio: *Tell Me* (BOA Editions, USA, 2000). **Agha Shahid Ali:** *The Half-Inch Himalayas* (Wesleyan University Press, 1987). **Yehuda Amichai:** 'The Place Where We Are Right' and 'A Man in His Life' from *The Selected Poetry of Yehuda Amichai*, tr. Chana Bloch & Stephen Mitchell (HarperCollins, 1986; rev. ed. University of California Press, 1996), by permission of the University of California Press; 'The Diameter of the Bomb' from *Selected Poems*, ed. Ted Hughes & Daniel Weissbort (Faber & Faber, 2000). **W.H. Auden:** *Collected Poems*, ed. Edward Mendelson (Faber & Faber, 1991), by permission of Curtis Brown, New York.

Mourid Barghouti: *Midnight and other poems*, tr. Radwa Ashour (Arc, 2008). **Elizabeth Bishop:** *Complete Poems 1927-1979* (Farrar, Straus and Giroux, 1983), copyright © 1979, 1983 by Alice Helen Methfessel, by permission of Farrar, Straus and Giroux, LLC. **John Burnside:** 'Unwittingly' from *The Light Trap* (Jonathan Cape, 2002), part I of 'Of Gravity and Light', from *The Light Trap* (Jonathan Cape, 2002), by permission of the Random House Group Ltd.

Edip Cansever: *Dirty August*, tr. Julia Clare Tillinghast & Richard Tillinghast (Talisman House, USA, 2009), by permission of the translators. **Raymond Carver:** *All of Us: Collected Poems* (Harvill Press, 1996), by permission of Random House Group Ltd, copyright © 1996 Tess Gallagher. **Nina Cassian:** *Life Sentence: Selected Poems*, ed. William Jay Smith (Anvil Press Poetry, 1990). **Charles Causley:** *Collected Poems 1951-2000* (Picador, 2000), by permission of David Higham Associates Ltd. **C.P. Cavafy:** *Collected Poems*, revised edition, tr. Edmund Keeley & Philip Sherrard (Chatto & Windus, 1998). **Julius Chingono:** 'As I Go', from *Poetry International Web* (Zimbabwe Domain, 2008), by permission of Poetry International on behalf of the estate of Julius Chingono. **Kate Clanchy:** *Newborn* (Picador, 2004), by permission of Macmillan Publishers Ltd. **Michael Coady:** *Two for a Woman, Three for a Man* (1980) by kind permission of Michael Coady and the Gallery Press, Loughcrew, Oldcastle, Co. Meath, Ireland. **David Constantine:** *Collected Poems* (Bloodaxe Books, 2004).

Imtiaz Dharker: *I Speak for the Devil* (Bloodaxe Books, 2001). **Michael Donaghy:** *Collected Poems* (Picador, 2009), by permission of Macmillan Publishers Ltd. **Mark Doty:** *Atlantis* (Jonathan Cape, 1996), by permission of the Random House Group Ltd. **Rita Dove:** *On the Bus with Rosa Parkes* (W.W. Norton & Company, 1999). **Alan Dugan:** *Poems Seven: New and Complete Poetry* (Seven Stories Press, NY, 2001). **Helen Dunmore:** *Out of the Blue: Poems 1975-2001* (Bloodaxe Books, 2001). **Stephen Dunn:** *Between Angels* (W.W. Norton & Company, New York, 1989).

T.S. Eliot: *The Complete Poems and Plays* (Faber & Faber, 1969).

U.A. Fanthorpe: *New & Collected Poems* (Enitharmon Press, 2010). **Robert Frost:** *The Poetry of Robert Frost*, ed. Edward Connery Lathem (Jonathan Cape, 1967), by permission of Random House Group Ltd.

Jack Gilbert: *Transgressions: Selected Poems* (Bloodaxe Books, 2006). **Dana Gioia:** *Daily Horoscope* (Graywolf Press, 1986). **Lars Gustafsson:** *A Time in Xanadu*, tr. John Irons (Copper Canyon Press, 2008), www.coppercanyonpress.org.

Kerry Hardie: 'Sheep Fair Day' from *Selected Poems* (Gallery Press/Bloodaxe Books, 2011), reprinted from *The Sky Didn't Fall* (Gallery Press, 2003), by permission of The Gallery Press. **Seamus Heaney:** *Opened Ground: Poems 1966-1996* (Faber & Faber, 1998). **Geoffrey Hill:** *Collected Poems* (Penguin, 1985). **Nâzim Hikmet:** *Poems of Nâzim Hikmet*, tr. Randy Blasing & Mutlu Konuk (Persea Books, Inc, NY, 1994; second edition, 2002). **Jane Hirshfield:** 'The Weighing' from *Each Happiness Ringed by Lions: Selected Poems* (Bloodaxe Books, 2005); 'Burlap Sack' from *After* (Bloodaxe Books, 2006). **Miroslav Holub:** *Poems Before & After: Collected English Translations*, second edition (Bloodaxe Books, 2006). **Langston Hughes:** *The Collected Poems of Langston Hughes* (Alfred A. Knopf, Inc, 1994), by permission of David Higham Associates.

Mohja Kahf: *E-mails from Scheherazad* (University of Florida Press, 2003).

Jaan Kaplinski: *Selected Poems* (Bloodaxe Books, 2011). **Doris Kareva:** *Shape of Time*, tr. Tiina Aleman (Arc, 2010). **Jackie Kay:** *Darling: New & Selected Poems* (Bloodaxe Books, 2007). **Brendan Kennelly:** *Familiar Strangers: New & Selected Poems 1960-2004* (Bloodaxe Books, 2004). **Jane Kenyon:** *Let Evening Come: Selected Poems* (Bloodaxe Books, 2005), copyright © 2005 Estate of

INDEX OF WRITERS

INDEX OF TITLES